Ask Ali

A guide to:

ABU DHABI

With compliments of:

A Mubadala Aerospace, Sikorsky and Lockheed Martin Company

Third edition
ISBN978-9948-15-588-1

Illustrations by Kagan McLeod

Photographs supported by Emarat Alyoum

Ask-Ali.com Inc
P.O. Box 75858, Abu Dhabi, United Arab Emirates
Phone: 02 641 9914   Fax: 02 641 9915
Email: ali@ask-ali.com   Web: www.ask-ali.com

Shukran jazeelan to the Ask Ali Team.

The Capital
العـــاصمه

Welcome

Dear Guest,

Many people are now choosing to live all over the world and the resulting mix of cultures is part of the beauty of globalization. We might have different tastes, but we still agree on certain values such as respect for each other's differences. Whether you are a tourist, a business traveler or a resident, I want to welcome you. You are now our friends and we want to take care of you and share our culture, heritage and future with you. This is your home too.

The UAE stands at a fascinating place in its history. Abu Dhabi is one of the fastest growing metropolitan cities in the world and a growing cultural force in the Middle East, yet the city still holds dear the tribal past and religious ideals on which it was founded. This humble guide is meant to enrich your knowledge of the city, the country and us Emiratis, so that you can better understand your new friends in the Middle East.

I am so grateful the first edition of *Ask Ali: A guide to Abu Dhabi* helped and welcomed thousands of visitors and residents to embrace Abu Dhabi. I will always say this: consider me your first local friend. I am happy to be there for you at any time, so take advantage of this offer. And remember whenever you have any concerns or questions, ask Ali. That's me, and, yes, I will answer.

Hayakom Allah

About Ali

Garfield once said that all the cute kittens go to Abu Dhabi, but I want you to know the people here are pretty nice too – not to mention the puppies. My master, Ali, has a soft spot for animals. He also loves meeting new people and has a passion for showing visitors around his country and sharing his heritage. My master is one of the fastest-rising media personalities in the Gulf, and I'm so proud of him. Ali has been guiding people for quite some time now, but he's still new to writing it all down. Ever since the first edition of this book was published, my master has been on to bigger things. He was nominated to the Ahlan Hot 100 personalities of 2011 list. Furthermore, the Environment Agency – Abu Dhabi asked Ali to become their environmental ambassador in the UAE. Master Ali always takes it upon himself to personally advocate for animals and care for the environment, so this was indeed an honor for him.

I recommend that you check him out on the online portal www.onetvo.com – I'm even featured in one episode. Or visit his website, www.ask-ali.com, and ask my master any questions you might have about the region.

Woof! Woof! - **Saluki**

About Saluki

Meet my good buddy, Saluki. He will be joining us on our journey through Abu Dhabi and the UAE. Our ancestors depended on the saluki to hunt gazelles and rabbits because they have amazing endurance and can reach speeds of up to 45kph. Back in those days, the saluki was relied upon to provide food for survival, so I thought he was the perfect way to introduce you to the animals we cherish in the UAE. Plus, he kept bugging me to be in the book. You might know that we spend a lot of money and time on horses and camels, but we do this because we really care about animals.

The saluki is here to bring a smile to your face, but also to remind people of the great passion we have for our animals. Learn about the saluki, falcon, horse or camel and you'll never run out of conversation starters with locals.

One of my top duties in life is animal welfare, and awareness of this issue is just starting to spread, which is a positive sign. I am working closely with the authorities to get citizens and residents of Abu Dhabi to embrace more pets and abandoned animals. I'd like to see as many people as possible involved in this cause with me.

- Ali

A guide to this guide

The feedback I received following the launch of the first edition of this guide was absolutely phenomenal (Alhamdulillah). Here I am again, publishing a second, updated edition to welcome new friends as always.

Whether you are a tourist, business traveler, planning to move here or already live here, I hope this miniguide helps you enjoy your time in Abu Dhabi. Even locals could learn a thing or two because I have included both my personal recommendations and those of my expat friends.

Please be aware that I am not advertising any of the places in this guide. Furthermore, Abu Dhabi is changing at such a fast pace that some new establishments might not have been included, while some of my all-time favorites could have closed.

The first thing you might notice is the sketch of me saying "Psst." This signifies that I (or Saluki) am offering up some local knowledge, so be sure to take note.

You will also notice the special Arabic-inspired designs of these pages, which are meant to give you a sense of our Arab aesthetic.

When I am describing a venue, I have included the details I think you will need, for example:

Marina Mall

a website for the technologically inclined

www.marinamall.ae; 02 681 2310;

a phone number

Breakwater Area

a landmark near the place, the area or the street name

This is to make sure that you know the way locals refer to different locations, where often streets do not have a name (or they have three!), buildings are not numbered, and navigation is achieved using landmarks.

Born and raised in the United Arab Emirates, I am naturally biased in my love and devotion for this small land in the Gulf, which has unconditionally given, and continues to give, a grand and bountiful quality of life to its citizens.

Abu Dhabi is among the world's highest ranked cities in terms of personal safety and lifestyle.

This is all a reality by design; a testament to the hard work, love, and dedication of our venerated leaders. This country continues to grow by leaps and bounds creating undulating waves of progress that are felt on a global scale.

It is this love, gratitude, and appreciation that drives me and my brethren to flourish in this booming oasis, and the reason why I would like all of you to get to know My Emirates! My UAE! My Abu Dhabi! I urge each and all to learn about the UAE culture and history on a personal level, and get to know it like the Emaratis do.

'Ask Ali,' is a perfect example of the devotion people feel for this nation and their desire to share it with the entire world.

My God, the Almighty, continue to bless this land, its leaders, and all its inhabitants towards achieving greater prosperity for all mankind.

Fahed Al Shamesi
Chief Executive Officer
AMMROC

Getting acquainted

Contents

Getting acquainted

History

Even though the UAE is a young country, it has an intriguing history. Before oil was discovered in the 1940s, Emiratis made their money pearling, which was a very dangerous trade.

At one point in the late 19th century, there were 1,200 pearling boats operating in Abu Dhabi, Dubai and Ras al Khaimah. To get the pearls, men would dive to the bottom of the Gulf to find oysters. Pearl diving called for physical endurance and mental fortitude and resulted in villages being without able-bodied men for long periods. The Japanese discovered a method to culture pearls that made pearl divers redundant, but fortunately this coincided with the discovery of oil in the 1940s and 1950s. Because of its proximity to India and Iran, this area was also important for shipping and trading.

Each emirate started out as a dynasty and there were many disagreements. A turning point came in 1853, when the leaders of several sheikhdoms signed a treaty referring all future disputes to the United Kingdom.

The British influenced much of our history, sometimes strategically in order to keep their European rivals away. In an 1892 treaty, they agreed to protect the sheikhdoms that, in return, would not enter into relationships with other governments.

The country's fortunes took a dramatic turn with the discovery of oil and the ascension of Sheikh Zayed bin Sultan Al Nahyan to Ruler of Abu Dhabi. Sheikh Zayed inspired the leaders of the other emirates to form a council to co-ordinate policies. This council took on greater significance when Britain reduced its presence in the late 1960s and left in the early 1970s. With no foreign protection, the leaders of the emirates met to discuss a union. On December 2, 1971, my country was born.

In Sheikh Zayed's lifetime, the country went from seven sparse tribal territories protected by the British to a wealthy independent nation with considerable influence in the Middle East. Our beloved leader passed away in 2004 and the country officially mourned his death for two weeks.

His eldest son, HH Sheikh Khalifa bin Zayed Al Nahyan, succeeded him as Ruler of Abu Dhabi and President of the UAE. HH Sheikh Mohammed bin Zayed Al Nahyan succeeded HH Sheikh Khalifa as the Crown Prince of Abu Dhabi and Deputy Supreme Commander of the UAE Armed Forces. The Vice President and Ruler of Dubai is HH Sheikh Mohammed bin Rashid Al Maktoum.

The late Sheikh Zayed bin Sultan Al Nahyan

National anthem

Our national anthem gives me chills every time I recite it. After all, we are a patriotic people. Below is the English translation of our anthem and, as you can see, it is all about sacrificing and giving back to our beloved country. Private and Government schools recite the national anthem every day. Try practicing it with your children when you can. Below each line of the English translation is how it is recited in anglicized Arabic.

Live my country, the unity of our Emirates lives
(E'eshy biladi, asha etihadu emaratina)

You have lived for a nation
(Eshti lisha'ben)

Whose religion is Islam and guide is the Quran
(Dinahul Islamu, hadyahul quranu)

I made you stronger in God's name oh homeland
(Hassantuka bismillah ya watan)

My country, my country, my country, my country
(Biladi Biladi Biladi Biladi)

God has protected you from the evils of the time
(Hamaki Al illah shuroor alzaman)

We have sworn to build and work
(Aqsamna an nabni ya n'amal)

Work sincerely, work sincerely
(N'amal nokhles, N'amal nokhles)

As long as we live, we'll be sincere, sincere
(Mahma eshna nokhles nokhles)

The safety has lasted and the flag has lived oh our Emirates
(Dam al amanu wa ash al 'alam ya Emaratina)

The symbol of Arabism
(Ramz ul 'orubati)

We all sacrifice for you, we supply you with our blood
(Kulluna Nafdeeki, Bel dima narweeki)

We sacrifice for you with our souls oh homeland
(Nafdeeka bel arwah ya watan)

Attitudes toward Government

HH Sheikh Mohammed bin Rashid Al Maktoum

HH Sheikh Khalifa bin Zayed Al Nahyan

The late Sheikh Zayed bin Sultan Al Nahyan

HH Sheikh Moha bin Zayed Al Na

Although we are not a democracy, we strongly believe that our Government has our best interests at heart and will listen to our concerns. We are passionately patriotic by nature, as you will notice on National Day. We put up pictures of our rulers to show our love and respect for the men who built our country. This is in keeping with our tribal past and our Arabic heritage. A leader commanded the loyalty of his tribe, but he had to lead by consensus. If he lost the confidence of his tribe, he could be unceremoniously deposed. The late Sheikh Zayed could not have said it any better when he stated: "Our system of Government does not derive its authority from man, but is enshrined in our religion and is based on God's book, the holy Quran. What need have we of what others have conjured up? Its teachings are eternal and complete, while the systems conjured up by man are transitory and incomplete." I believe this explains why our Government has been successful in bringing many nationalities together.

Psst...

If you display portraits of our leaders in your office, Emirati visitors will notice them and understand that you share the vision and goals of the country.

As a guideline, if there are two portraits, the most significant one goes on the right. If there are three, the main one is in the middle, with the next significant person to his left, and the following significant person to his right. For instance, in Abu Dhabi, the order from left to right will be: HH Sheikh Khalifa bin Zayed Al Nahyan who is the President of the UAE and Ruler of Abu Dhabi, then the late Sheikh Zayed bin Sultan Al Nahyan, the founder of the country, then Sheikh Mohammed bin Zayed, the Crown Prince of Abu Dhabi. In Government offices in Abu Dhabi you are also likely to see photographs of Sheikh Mohammed bin Rashid Al Maktoum, because he is not only the Ruler of Dubai but also the Vice President and Prime Minister of the UAE. He is placed on the left side of Sheikh Khalifa. In other emirates you will see photos of their respective leaders and crown princes.

Here is a list of the rulers and crown princes of the rest of the emirates:
DUBAI - HH Sheikh Mohammed bin Rashid Al Maktoum
Crown Prince - HH Sheikh Hamdan bin Mohammed Al Maktoum
SHARJAH - HH Dr Sheikh Sultan bin Mohammed Al Qasimi
Crown Prince - HH Sheikh Mohammed bin Sultan Al Qasimi
AJMAN - HH Sheikh Humaid bin Rashid Al Nuaimi
Crown Prince - HH Sheikh Ammar bin Humaid Al Nuaimi
UMM AL QAIWAIN - HH Sheikh Saud bin Rashid Al Mu'alla
Crown Prince - HH Sheikh Rashid bin Saud Al Mu'alla
RAS AL KHAIMAH - HH Sheikh Saud bin Saqr Al Qasimi
Crown Prince - HH Sheikh Mohammed bin Saud Al Qasimi
FUJAIRAH - HH Sheikh Hamad bin Mohammed Al Sharqi
Crown Prince - HH Sheikh Mohammed bin Hamad Al Sharqi

Geography

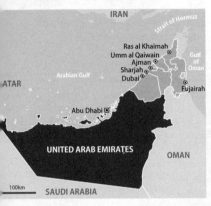

My country lies on the very south of the Arabian Gulf on a peninsula. It is made up of seven emirates – like states or sheikhdoms – including Abu Dhabi, the capital. Abu Dhabi has a population of 1.5 million and is the largest Emirate by land area. Dubai, the UAE's most populated city at about 2.5 million, is about a one-and-a-half-hour drive to the north east. If you continue driving ahead you will pass through Sharjah, Ajman, Umm al Qaiwain and Ras al Khaimah. Fujairah is due east from Dubai.

To the south and west, the UAE shares with Saudi Arabia a border and the Empty Quarter, which is a vast expanse of empty desert that contains some of the world's largest sand dunes. Oman is our eastern neighbor, and across the Arabian Gulf, to the north, is Iran.

Altogether, the UAE covers 83,600 square kilometers, 80 per cent of which is desert. But we also have mountains and oases as well as more than 200 islands.

Climate

Sell your parka, you won't be needing it in the UAE. For most of the year you will encounter nothing but sunshine and warm temperatures. Still, I would like to clarify a few misconceptions about the climate here. Although my country is 80 per cent desert, the city of Abu Dhabi is located on an island, therefore the air becomes quite humid, especially in the summer months of June through September when temperatures reach upward of 45°C. We also get rain and in the last couple of years even snow (in the mountains, but it still counts!) It doesn't rain a lot, a maximum of a couple of weeks every year, and almost all of it in January, February and March, but it does happen. It also can get chilly on winter nights, with the thermometer dropping to 10°C. We also get sandstorms from winds known as the Shamal (which means north). For the rest of the year expect temperatures between 20°C and 35°C.

Faith

While the UAE is tolerant of other religions, the teachings of the holy Quran inform much of our behavior. If, for instance, you are an alcohol drinker, we don't expect you to quit drinking or stop other customs you might practice back home, but it is important that expatriates respect our religious codes.

We will touch on religion more in later sections, but a good place to start is with the basics. You should get to know the terminology. Islam is the religion and Islamic is the adjective used to describe a country or a law. Muslims are the followers of Islam. The proper pronunciation of the word is "moss-lim", not "muzz-lim".

Islam has more than one billion followers, but less than 10 per cent of them are Arabs. The word Islam comes from an Arabic word meaning peace and submission to God. Islam teaches that one can only find

Psst...

You might have noticed that people use the acronym PBUH after Prophet Mohammed's name. In Islam, we do this to signify our devotion to the final prophet of Allah. The acronym stands for Peace Be Upon Him. We also make sure to say this after mentioning other prophets such as Issa (Jesus), Mosa (Moses), Ibrahim (Abraham) and Nooh (Noah). The holy Quran is the Islamic holy book, but we also follow the advice Prophet Mohammed (PBUH) gave us in the form of hadiths, which are statements he made, and sunnas, which are practices he followed that have been passed down. Don't worry – if you are a non-Muslim, you're not expected to say PBUH, but it is always appreciated if you do.

peace in life by submitting to Almighty God (Allah) in heart, soul and deed. It is considered one of the Abrahamic, monotheistic faiths, along with Judaism and Christianity.

National dress

Our clothes address our faith's call for modesty, but they are also influenced by our scorching climate and social norms. Men traditionally wear breathable, loose robes to the ankle known as kandouras. We also cover our heads with a ghutra, a square scarf made of cotton folded into a triangular shape with the folded part placed on the forehead. The scarf is secured with a small white cap (tagiya or gahfiya) underneath and a black cord (ogal) on top.

In the past the ogal was used to tie a camel's legs together so it wouldn't run off. We also usually wear sandals, for two reasons: they are cool for the feet and easy to remove at the mosque.

The flowing black gown worn by Emirati women is known as the abaya and suits our concern for women's modesty. Black cloth protects skin from sunburn and is also harder to see through, allowing the fabric to be thinner and cooler without being revealing. But I suspect the main reason why today's young women wear it is because it makes them look slim! The sheila is the cloth, usually black, that loosely covers a woman's head and sometimes her face – the fabric is lightweight so a woman can see through it. Some women wear a niqab, which leaves only a slit for the eyes. In

some countries this is called a burqa but we use that word to refer to the face mask that used to be worn when a woman got married. Today, you mostly see older women in the Gulf wearing the burqa.

Tourist shops sell ready-made kandouras and abayas, but if you want properly fitted Gulf clothing, I advise you to visit one of our talented tailors.

For gentlemen, the best of these shops will simply take your measurements and your mobile number, and, presto, you'll have a perfectly tailored kandoura for between Dhs100 and Dhs300.

Ladies wear abayas and sheilas on top of their regular clothes when they go out of the house. A tailor-made abaya will cost between Dhs300 and Dhs5,000 depending on the textile, embroidery and design you choose. Some women use

Psst...

In the winter, we wear thicker materials such as wool and darker colors. My personal favorite is brown, which makes me look particularly handsome. I hope brown becomes the official kandoura color for tourist guides one day.

jewels and crystals to complete their look. Talk to your female Emirati colleagues, who always look beautiful. With their recommendation you will get a better price.

Ghanati
Muroor Road, 02 441 8666
Ghanati is a brand that is popular with the locals here for their kandouras, abayas and jalabiyas for women. Pay them a visit to get your custom-made clothing.

Khalidiya Street
Behind Al Muhairi Center
This street is dedicated to selling abayas, jalabiyas (a dress usually worn to entertain guests at home) and Arabic perfumes and sweets. You can find ready-to-wear or tailor-made abayas according to your style and size.

3abaya
www.3abaya.com
The first online portal (who said we weren't modern?) dedicated to selling abayas by prominent regional designers.

Psst...

Did you notice the number 3 before the word abaya? Since Arabic has letters and pronunciations that are not found in the Latin alphabet, we have come up with creative ways to use numbers to signify these Arabic letters. While some language institutions have come up with their own usages, the ones I recommend are listed in the glossary on page 240.

For example, the letter "ع" in Arabic which is pronounced as "Ain" is equal to the number "3" in internet language; so Ali = 3li. These numbers correspond to the similar shapes of Arabic letters, which makes it easier to understand.

Remember to pack

Cottons and linens will be your friends in the summer. Invest in a hat to keep the sun off your head and don't forget a good pair of sunglasses. Abu Dhabi's sun shines bright, so you will be able to wear your shades at least 300 days a year. I also recommend slip-on shoes or sandals to cope with the hot weather and because you will usually be expected to remove your footwear prior to entering an Emirati's home. I would also recommend sunscreen with a minimum SPF of 20.

During the winter months, warmer clothing is recommended – long sleeves, sweaters and light jackets – for the cool evenings and chilly mornings.

Psst...

Emiratis make up less than 20 per cent of the population. It's nearly impossible for an expat to tell, say, an Omani man from an Emirati, nor do we expect you to. Just try to remember not to make judgments based on assumptions. Badmouthing anyone, Emirati or not, is unacceptable. We are quite sensitive about this, especially since saving face is so important in our community.

Also...

Bling is not our thing when it comes to men's style. Excessive jewelry on men is frowned upon, although watches and wedding rings are fine. You won't see Muslim men in gold chains, bracelets or earrings (and definitely not eyebrow piercings!) because Islam sees them as immodest and effeminate.

Expat dress code

If you dress modestly, locals will appreciate your sensitivity to our culture. While some people flout these unofficial rules, trust me, we do not approve. This is not to say you will go to jail for wearing a short skirt. But you need to think about how to dress and behave appropriately in certain areas. Honestly, it's mostly common sense.

You will often see signs at the entrances to shopping malls regarding modesty, which help illustrate appropriate behavior. Avoid images on clothing that we find disrespectful, such as silhouettes of naked women or the middle finger.

Men:
1. Always wear a shirt in public.
2. Avoid shorts above the knee, except at the beach and the gym.
3. Suits or jackets with collared shirts and trousers are appropriate business attire.

Women:
1. Keep arms covered preferably to the elbow.
2. Avoid low-cut necklines or exposed knees.
3. For business, skirts should not be too tight and shirts should not be transparent.

Attitudes toward women

More and more Emirati women are taking on leadership roles and delving into entrepreneurship. Our foreign trade minister is a woman, HE Sheikha Lubna Al Qasimi. Many Emirati women have important posts as ambassadors, judges, school principals, rally-car drivers and even an Olympic tae kwon do competitor, Sheikha Maitha bint Mohammed bin Rashid Al Maktoum.

Women graduates significantly outnumber men, which is a tribute to the late Sheikh Zayed who insisted on an equal education policy many years ago.

A woman's privacy is highly valued; governmental organizations and banks have dedicated customer service lines or separate branches to help women avoid long queues. Many restaurants, cafes and food courts also have separate rooms for families.

Psst...

You may find that most Emirati women prefer not to shake the hands of men and the reverse may also be true. Do not be offended; this is our custom. It is also not recommended to smile at strangers of the opposite gender, as it could be misinterpreted. Like many things here, however, it depends on the context and the place; how you dress, how old you are, where you are at the time and whether or not your smile looks merely friendly or more like, "Hey, baby". Without permission from an Emirati woman, it would be impolite and inappropriate to approach her to talk, but if there is a reason for your interaction – her abaya is on fire, or she left her cellphone in a cafe – then that's fine. You can try offering an accepting and friendly smile, a warm and gentle "Hello" or "As salamu alaykum" (see page 230), but if she does not react, then it's a sign of no, thank you.

There are also some gender-specific rules that are intrinsic to our culture. For example, a man should never let his mother, sister or wife carry bags when his hands are empty (OK, maybe if it's my sister).

Relationships with women are undertaken carefully. We speak to women very respectfully, so you might sense there is a gap between the sexes, but to us this gap equals respect.

Many of us have lived in other countries, so we understand that women in most other parts of the world do not live like our women. We respect this. The best advice I could give to female expats is that if you show the requisite modesty our culture calls for, you will have no problems in our country.

Tips for female visitors

It can be daunting for women to travel to a foreign land alone, especially if they don't know much about the culture. Misconceptions and stereotypes exist everywhere, including the Middle East, so it is important that you come across as respectable at all times.

Although the UAE is relatively open about certain things, it is best to keep the following tips in mind if you want to avoid being misunderstood:

1. To avoid being hit on, it is advisable to wear a ring on your finger, even if you are not married or engaged.

2. Don't stare at men because they could take it as a hint that you're offering something.

3. If someone is throwing about rude or weird comments, do your best to ignore it – don't give them the time of day. They will get tired and leave.

4. When riding in taxis or buses alone, never sit next to the driver unless she is female.

5. Avoid saying that you are visiting the country by yourself. It is better to say you're here with some friends or family.

6. If you need help, alert the nearest security guard or police officer.

7. Be aware of how flirtatious you may act. People here perceive the slightest gestures as something serious. So always be careful of the image you project of yourself.

8. In restaurants, we also have family sections, which are reserved for women or couples with children. Feel free to ask to be seated there if you are uncomfortable with the environment.

9. If you are running errands and have to stand in queues, ask where the ladies queue is. It should be much shorter and will save you from being sandwiched between men.

10. God forbid you feel like someone is about to harass you, but if this happens call 999 and be sure to talk loud enough to be understood. Try to get to a place quickly where there are many people.

11. If you are here with your significant other, you may find it easier to refer to him as your fiancé or spouse when introducing him to Arabs or Emirati families.

12. When in public, try not to laugh so loudly that it attracts a lot of attention. It is impolite and also disturbs people who may feel too shy to ask you to keep it down.

Psst...

New baby? Congratulations. A quick heads-up on breastfeeding in the UAE. We understand how important this is for new mothers, but you might find it difficult to find private breastfeeding rooms in public spaces. This is changing gradually as the new malls popping up here start to offer the service. On the other hand, almost every restaurant and cafe will have a family section where you are free to breastfeed. Just try to remember the conservative nature of our society and be discreet.

Cohabitation

We understand that living with a member of the opposite sex in many countries does not necessarily mean you are dating. Islam, however, states that men and women who are not related should not live together and as our laws follow our religion, cohabitation is illegal in the UAE. If you have friends or family of the opposite sex visiting, they are more than welcome to stay with you.

Censorship

If we cover ourselves out of modesty, you can imagine how we feel about nudity in the media. All cinema releases go through Government censors, who edit out risqué scenes. Similarly, offensive content is blacked out of magazines and blocked on the internet. Remember this when packing. When you arrive, your DVDs, CDs, books, magazines or computer may be confiscated temporarily for the content to be checked.

Psst...

We welcome people of all faiths into our country, so it is not illegal to bring your religion's holy book or objects, such as a cross or a Buddha statue. One of the central tenets of Islam is our belief in God, and the existence of people with other religions is a matter of respect.

Books bought outside the UAE are not immune to this law. It is also illegal to defame any member of the ruling families of any of the emirates.

Drugs

In most western countries recreational drugs are illegal, but the law is rarely enforced for small amounts. Let's get something straight – this is not the case in the UAE. Leave your drugs at home. In fact, don't even think about using them before you arrive; customs officials may require new arrivals to take a blood test.

You should also check to see if your prescriptions are allowed here. Many sleeping pills, psychiatric drugs and opiates such as codeine are banned or tightly regulated. You might be required to show your prescription upon entering the UAE.

Alcohol and cigarettes

Abu Dhabi allows alcohol for non-Muslims, but with certain limitations. You may drink in designated bars and clubs, which are usually located in hotels, and in the privacy of your home. You must obtain a liquor license (page 117) and may be asked to show this by the authorities. Above all, please show respect for our culture. Alcohol is forbidden in Islam, but we allow it for our guests to help them feel welcome. Don't abuse our good faith (there is a law against public drunkenness). Drink in moderation and arrange for safe transportation home. Drunk driving is also illegal and may lead to jail time.

You can bring four liters of alchohol into the UAE, as well as 400 cigarettes and Dhs3,000 worth of cigars.

Pets

With the influx of expatriates in the UAE, Emiratis are slowly getting used to the idea of people having animals as part of their families. It would be great if newcomers would try to understand our sensitivities as well. Our attitude toward animals differs from that of westerners. We love animals, but don't interact with them inside our homes because of hygiene reasons. We respect all of God's creatures, even pigs. We just don't eat that particular animal.

Psst...

Instead of bringing your pet from home, you can adopt one when you get here. Strays of Abu Dhabi is a charity that rescues and rehabilitates abandoned dogs, and Feline Friends does the same for cats. Both groups ensure that abandoned pets receive proper veterinary care and vaccinations before assessing their personality in order to make a good match with a new owner. It is advisable to have a microchip implanted in your pet because the microchip has a unique ID code that helps authorities identify lost pets. It is also required for international travel. Clinics such as The British Veterinary Centre offer microchipping services. For detailed information, log on to www.britvet.com or call 02 665 0085.

Abu Dhabi Animal Shelter
www.abudhabianimalshelter.com; 02 5755155; 800 1122

Feline Friends
www.felinefriendsuae.com; 050 823 1569; 050 582 2916 (emergency)

Petz n' Stuff
www.petznstuff.com; 050 516 1020

If you want to "click" with an Emirati, good topics of conversation involve the animals we admire. If you know anything about camels or falconry, a local will be impressed because this is rare. Or if you've had experience hunting with dogs, we'd love to talk about that. My sister has a German shepherd called Junior, but I can't picture any Emirati family raising a chihuahua. To us, dogs are for guarding and hunting.

We understand that animals need to do their business, so owners should avoid walking their dogs around mosques. The last thing that a worshipper should have to worry about is stepping on dog waste. Another consideration is the time you choose to take your dog for a walk. Try to avoid taking Rover out at prayer time near a mosque as his bark could distract the faithful.

Psst...

Remember, the temperature here reaches 45°C in the summer, which might be too hot for your furry friend. All animals entering the UAE must have a health certificate and vaccination records.

Jobs

The UAE's economy has promising career opportunities, but we also have certain business attitudes you should know about before arriving. A majority of the executives who work here have been headhunted. Job searches can be difficult because Arabs like to do business with those they trust, meaning those they know or with whom they have friends in common. We don't like to do business over the phone or without initially meeting you. This goes back to our nomadic roots when we needed to trust our fellow tribe members just to survive.

Psst...

The three most important things to consider when job hunting in this country are relationships, relationships and relationships. By all means apply online. I respect this method and think it's a good start. But don't expect an immediate response unless the company needs someone right away. This is just to get your résumé out there. What you want to do is to follow this up with an e-mail to the HR department asking for a meeting. You just want to sit with them, get into their office. The minute they see you, shake your hand and offer you tea or coffee, you're halfway there because you have established a relationship. Even if it doesn't work out with that company, they might recommend you to someone else who is hiring.

Free trade zones

No, I don't mean the place to shop for bargains on perfume and electronics, but rather a Government initiative to attract more investment from foreign countries. Free zones are a recent driving force of Abu Dhabi's growth because they permit firms located there to be 100 per cent foreign owned, pay no corporate tax and are allowed total repatriation of capital and profits. Attractive, isn't it? Examples of free zones are Masdar, twofour54, ICAD and more.

For a list of free trade zones in Abu Dhabi, visit www.ask-ali.com.

Starting a business

So you've come to Abu Dhabi and had an epiphany on how to make money. Don't worry, Abu Dhabi has many opportunities for start-ups of all kinds. What matters is that you have finally decided to venture out on your own. My advice, before you start with the paperwork, is to make sure of one thing: that you research the local market very well.

It's important to know how your business can cater to the local market and help it grow.

Psst...

You started a business, and you're looking for a partner, sponsor, funding, acquisitions, advisory services, etc. Consider "Connections ME" as the party that can take care of all this for you with local know-how. It is a foreign company representation firm with offices in the UK and Abu Dhabi. (www.connectionsme.com)

The Abu Dhabi Chamber of Commerce offers a range of services for new and established companies. For more information, visit its website, www.abudhabichamber.ae.

Visas

While citizens of many countries will need to apply for a visa before they arrive in the UAE, several nationalities are eligible for a visitor's visa upon arrival. This allows for a stay of up to 30 days, albeit extendable on terms and conditions. Certain nationalities can get a free tourist visa upon arrival at the airport.

Please be aware that rules and regulations can change, so always check with your embassy first to avoid a hassle.

If you happen to overstay your visa and you are a visitor without a job, you can be penalized a fee of Dhs100 per day. Check with your sponsor to make sure that you receive your visa within 30 days. This will be valid for three years if you work with a Government entity, and two years if you're employed by a private company. You will need a slightly different visa if your family is coming with you. You can only sponsor your family if you make over Dhs4,000 a month, though it is best to double check with your employer.

If you are employed in a free-zone area, the residency visa rules differ from that of companies that employ under a regular trade license. Be sure to check the laws and regulations of the specific free zone where you are based. You can contact them on their respective websites.

Psst...

Etihad now extends a very helpful visa service to those who fly with them and are not eligible for a visa on arrival. To apply for a visa to the UAE, you can log on to www.ttsuaevisas.com and follow their guidelines.

Medical regulations

When considering relocating to the UAE, it is crucial for you to know of our medical restrictions. People diagnosed with HIV/AIDS, tuberculosis, leprosy, or hepatitis B or C should check whether they can receive treatment here or are ineligible to stay in an effort to prevent further spread of these diseases.

My country is very clean, safe and has an advanced healthcare system. That being said, some visitors feel more comfortable getting their vaccinations from their general practitioner before arriving.

For a list of recommended vaccinations, visit www.mdtravelhealth.com.

Identity cards

www.emiratesid.ae

The Government launched the national ID card to streamline services and combat fraud.

I think it also makes all of us, expats and locals, feel more like one big, happy family by giving us a sense of, well, identity.

The card contains your electronic signature and photo and is mandatory for all Emiratis and expatriate residents. In some, but not all emirates, an ID card is required for some things such as license and registration services. For example, you cannot renew a driver's license or register your car in Abu Dhabi without having an ID card.

To register, go to the website and download the form. You will then need to arrange an appointment at one of the registration centers.

When you go, take your passport and some cash; it's Dhs100 for every year of your visa and another Dhs20 for a courier to deliver the card.

Psst...

The reason most Government agencies and employers ask for so many photographs is that almost everybody wants your picture here. We tend to go a bit overboard on the paperwork, but we really want to know all about you. An exception of this requirement is the Emirates ID. You do not need to take passport-size photos with you as they will take your picture while registering at the center. For children under 15 years of age, you will only have to take one passport-size picture with a light blue background.

Health insurance

Health insurance is mandatory in the UAE and employers must provide it and take care of the paperwork. In fact, you must have proof of health insurance before you can obtain a residence visa. After a blood test to prove you don't have HIV or hepatitis and a chest X-ray to prove you don't have tuberculosis, you will get your health card. Keep it on you at all times in case of emergency. The insurance company is called Daman (www.damanhealth.ae). See page 90 for a list of some of the city's best known hospitals.

Working hours

The work week in Abu Dhabi and across the country is Sunday to Thursday. Government office hours vary, and they usually finish earlier than private companies. Banks generally open at 7.30am and close at 1.30pm. Then they reopen at 5pm. Some street shops close in the afternoon but reopen until at least 10pm. Major malls tend to be open from 10am to 10pm and until midnight on weekends. Friday is the holy day for Muslims and many stores do not open until the late afternoon.

Psst...

A former expat boss of mine used to be amazed that her son's friends would knock on their door at 11pm to ask her son to play. What can I say? We're night owls. We do everything later, from meal time to bedtime. You will find that restaurants are open much later and movie theaters regularly screen films at midnight.

Getting acquainted

Public holidays

The UAE follows both the lunar and Gregorian calendars so the dates of most holidays change from year to year. The public holidays are:

Fixed dates
January 1 – New Year's Day
December 2 – National Day

Variable dates*
* The lunar calendar does not correspond with the Gregorian calendar, so the holidays normally change every year by 10 or 11 days earlier according to the sighting of the moon. The following are approximate estimates.

Al Mawled Al Nabawi – celebrates the day Prophet Mohammed (PBUH) was born. Muslims spend this day praying and reading the holy Quran. It falls on the 12th day of Rabi Al Awal.
2013 – January 24
2014 – January 14

Al Israa & Al Miraj – this holiday commemorates the ascension of the Prophet Mohammed (PBUH), also known as the night journey. It falls on the 27th of Rajab.
2013 – June 6
2014 – May 27

Ramadan – the last day of Ramadan is a holiday to prepare for Eid Al Fitr.
2013 – July 14
2014 – June 29

Eid Al Fitr – is the celebration of feasting after Ramadan. It lasts for three days.
2013 – August 14
2014 – July 29

Psst...

Gift giving is not mandatory when we celebrate our festive occasions. Greeting cards are commonly given to colleagues and friends. So don't think that it's too simple a gift.

Hajj – is the time when Muslims go on a pilgrimage to Mecca (Makkah). It is on the 9th day of Dhul Hijja.
2013 – October 14
2014 – October 4

Eid Al Adha – is celebrated the day after Hajj, and is known as the celebration of sacrifice. It lasts for four days.
2013 – October 15
2014 – October 5

Hijra – is the celebration of Islamic New year; it is celebrated on the first of Muharram.
2013 – November 5
2014 – October 25

Islamic Lunar Calendar

1 – Muharram
2 – Safar
3 – Rabi Al Awal
4 – Rabi Al Thani
5 – Jumada Al Awal
6 – Jumada Al Thani

7 – Rajab
8 – Sha'aban
9 – Ramadan
10 – Shawwal
11 – Dhul Qi'idah
12 – Dhul Hijjah

Money

Our currency is called the dirham and US$1 is equivalent to Dhs3.67. Each dirham is made up of 100 fils. We have five, 10 and 25 fil coins, but most of the coins you will see are 50 fils or one dirham. Notes come in denominations of 5, 10, 20, 50, 100, 200, 500 and, my favorite, 1,000.

Here is a list of goods to give you an idea of the approximate prices you will pay for everyday items in Abu Dhabi:

Can of soda – Dhs1.5
Liter of milk – Dhs6.5 to Dhs8
20 aspirin – Dhs13
Burger meal – Dhs15
Cinema ticket – Dhs35

Regular gas – Dhs1.72 per litre
500ml bottle of water – Dh1
Medium coffee – Dhs3 to Dhs12
Phone card – Dhs25
Newspaper – Dhs2 to Dhs10

Islamic banking

When exploring the city, you will notice signs for Islamic banks. The word Islamic does not mean they are exclusively for Muslims, as everyone is welcome to bank there.

Modern Islamic banking is founded on profit-sharing between lender and borrower. No interest is charged for borrowing money. The Arabic word for this is riba. Let me explain how loans work under this system. Instead of just giving you money to buy a car or house, the bank would actually buy the car or the house and sell it to you at a slightly higher price, which you pay in installments. The bank is not allowed to charge for late payments or increase the amount you are to pay.

There are more than 300 Islamic banks in more than 50 countries and even western financial institutions offering Islamic options. Much of modern capitalism originated from the Islamic Golden Age (the 8th to 13th centuries) when concepts such as mudaraba (speculation) and waqf (endowment) were introduced.

Banking and money transfers

Because the majority of the UAE's people are expatriates, it is common for them to send money back home. There are a number of competitively priced exchange centers that offer good prices for transferring money to your home country.

As well as Islamic financial institutions, we have internationally recognized banks such as HSBC, Citibank, Barclays, Lloyds and the Royal Bank of Scotland. Apart from banks, ATMs can be found throughout the city in malls, hotels, residential buildings and gas stations. Most major retailers accept credit cards, though there is sometimes a small service charge. The UAE mostly uses the signature system with credit cards, as opposed to the chip and pin system used in the UK, though it is being introduced slowly. In general, it's a good idea to carry cash at all times.

The best places to exchange money are in exchange centers since they offer the most updated rates, often even better than banks. They are all over the shopping malls in Abu Dhabi, so you will have no difficulty finding one. Most hotels will exchange money for you, but they don't normally accept large amounts. But if you're strapped for cash, you will be fine exchanging at the hotel.

Psst...

If a husband and wife have banking or money transfers to conduct, I strongly suggest the woman does it if the bank is crowded. If you're in a hurry, most banks have a women's section, which always has shorter lines.

Schools

Hurry, hurry, hurry! Don't waste a minute finding the right school for your children as the demand is incredibly high. The good news is that Abu Dhabi has schools for just about every curriculum. Due to the rapid growth in population over the past three decades, the UAE has been investing a lot of time, money and effort in order to offer world-class education from kindergarten to university. Recently, public schools introduced English-language instruction in addition to Arabic in certain subjects in order to prepare our next generation for a globalised world.

Abu Dhabi also offers schooling programs for children with special needs such as:

Al Noor Special Needs
02 449 3844; Muroor Road;
opposite to Emirates School

The Future Centre
www.future-centre.com; 02 666 9625;
Al Bateen area; Villa 250

Universities

As befitting a city that aims to be the Middle East's cultural hub, post-secondary education is seeing a renaissance in Abu Dhabi. Zayed University and Abu Dhabi University now accept expat students, and along with internationally renowned schools like New York University and Paris Sorbonne University, represent the international approach that was Sheikh Zayed's vision.

Abu Dhabi University
www.adu.ac.ae/en; 02 501 5555

Al Hosn University
www.alhosnu.ae; 02 407 0700

Masdar Institute of Science and Technology
www.masdar.ac.ae; 02 698 8122

New York University Abu Dhabi
www.nyuad.nyu.edu; 02 659 0740

Paris Sorbonne University
www.sorbonne.ae; 02 656 9555

Zayed University
www.zu.ac.ae; 02 599 3111

UAE University
www.uaeu.ac.ae; 03 755 5557

For more university options, visit www.ask-ali.com.

Psst...

Some government universities also welcome expats to enroll in their colleges. For example, Zayed University has now opened enrollment to expatriates and International students. UAE University also accepts expats, however, they must achieve a total grade of 90 per cent and above in their final exam from high school to qualify. So hurry and register your sons and daughters if you're looking for quality undergraduate education.

Cellphones

We love talking on the phone and staying connected through technology. When we leave home without our cellphones (which rarely happens), we feel like something is missing. If you like to talk on the phone then you have come to the right place!

When buying a phone, remember that they come with Arabic numbers and letters along with the Latin script. Most stores stock phones without the Arabic keypad if you don't need it, so ask if they offer what you want. Some of the kiosks that sell phone accessories in malls can change it for you. Just make sure to bargain!

You will also often encounter Arabic voicemail systems. Don't worry – you will have the option to proceed in English following the Arabic introduction.

To set up your phone before you get here, call the Government-operated Etisalat on +971 400 4101 or du on +971 55 567 8155. You can always recognize Etisalat service centers by the giant "golf ball" structures on top of their buildings. Some countries have roaming agreements with the UAE, but you can just as easily purchase a SIM card, which will give you a local number. Both post-paid and pay-as-you-go services exist.

Here is how you dial to check the credit balance on your phone:

Etisalat
Pre-Paid: *121#
GSM: 135

du
Pre-Paid: 135
GSM: *143#

Phoning home

When you want to call your loved ones to tell them what a great time you're having, remember that the UAE's time zone is GMT+4. The world clock (www.timeanddate.com/worldclock) will help to make sure you don't call them while they're asleep. Note, too, that we don't have daylight savings time here. Off-peak calling times are: Saturday-Thursday, 9pm-7am, all day Friday until Saturday 7am and all national public holidays. These times can change so watch out, although messages about such changes should come from the phone operators to your cellphone.

Emergency numbers

The three main emergency services' telephone numbers are easy to remember: fire is **997**, ambulance **998** and police **999**. Abu Dhabi traffic police officers wear dark blue and white uniforms.

Psst...

The UAE's international dialing code is +971. To call directory assistance, dial 181. You can usually tell where someone is calling from by the first two digits: 02 is Abu Dhabi, while 03 is Al Ain; 04 is Dubai; 06 is Ajman, Sharjah and Umm al Qaiwain; while 07 is Ras al Khaimah and 09 is Fujairah. To call landlines from other emirates, you have to add the emirate prefix to the seven-digit number.

Abu Dhabi International Airport

www.abudhabiairport.ae

The gateway to the capital of the UAE is an award-winning facility. It is located about a 20-30 minute drive from the heart of the city, and there are always plenty of taxis waiting to take you to your destination. Etihad Airways (www.etihadairways.com) is our award-winning airline that was set up as the national carrier of the UAE in 2003. It flies more than 100 international and regional routes, and seeks to reflect the best of Arabian hospitality (try the treats!) and to provide a relaxing experience that strives to make travel safe, efficient and within a friendly environment.

Psst...

Did you hear about the woman who went to the airport to shop? She heard they were having a lot of new arrivals. This is not far off when it comes to Abu Dhabi International Airport, which houses the world's leading luxury brands. So at least you'll have plenty to do if your flight is delayed. My colleague Shaima, who was a personal shopper, tells me that when entering a country, if you are transporting exotic items such as bags made of python skin, make sure to keep the certificate of manufacturing with you to ensure that it was made legally. All high-end brands that sell such exotic items are required to provide you with official documentation. So to be on the safe side, keep them handy.

Settling in

Contents

Settling in

Hotel apartments

These apartments might not be as glitzy as some of the five-star hotel franchises, but they are just as welcoming, good for accommodating lower budgets and better for longer stays because they often have kitchens in which you can make your own meals. There are plenty in the city, but here are some of the the most reputable ones. Most employers will put new expatriates up in a hotel apartment for a month or so until they find a new home.

Park Arjaan

www.rotana.com; 02 657 3333; near Khalifa Park
One of the newest hotel apartments in town. It's a few minutes' drive to several landmark venues close to Sheikh Zayed Mosque in Abu Dhabi, yet it's still not busy or noisy. The décor is modern and cosy. Take a stroll by Khalifa Park, which is walking distance from the hotel.

Cassells

www.cassellshotelapartments.ae; 02 610 7777; Electra Street
Located behind the Marks & Spencer building in the city center, Cassels offers 24-hour room service, a health club and business services. With all your basic needs taken care of, you can focus on getting to know your new city.

Phoenix Plaza Hotel Apartment

02 643 3322; Old Airport Road

I stumbled upon Phoenix Plaza by mistake the other day, only to find out that it is quite comfortable and very reasonably priced. The Chinese restaurant is one of the most authentic in Abu Dhabi as I did feel like I was in China with all the sizzling sounds, spicy aromas and the live cooking display.

Vision Hotel

www.visionhotel.net; 02 699 2666; Tourist Club area

Vision Hotel gets high ratings on online review sites, thanks to its modern rooms at reasonable prices. Rooms are available with kitchenettes, so you can make your own meals. The hotel also has a pool and fitness center.

Kingsgate

www.millenniumhotels.com; 02 499 5000; Tourist Club area

Within walking distance of Abu Dhabi Mall and the restaurants and bars of the Beach Rotana, the Kingsgate offers brand new rooms with a retro feel. While most rooms do not have kitchens – just a fridge and kettle – they provide excellent breakfast and there is 24-hour room service.

Ramec Guestline Hotel Apartments 1

www.rameehotels.com; 02 674 7000; Hamdan Street

Ramee has a mix of studio, one-bedroom and two-bedroom apartments. The rooms have modern facilities to make your stay comfortable and feel like home. The hotel apartments are conveniently located in the heart of Abu Dhabi city, close to major shopping malls and business areas.

For more accommodation options, visit www.ask-ali.com.

Hotels

Our hotels pride themselves on providing top-quality service and the utmost luxury. You do not have to spend a night to know what I mean; instead you may indulge in their spas, restaurants and other facilities to see for yourself.

Emirates Palace

www.emiratespalace.com; 02 690 9000; West Corniche
The landmark of the Middle East, as I like to call it, is operated by the luxury hotelier Kempinski Hotels and Resorts. Emirates Palace, known in Arabic as Qasr Al Emarat, is built in the style of a majestic palace rising from the desert. The facade is the color of sand and it boasts a staggering 114 domes covered in mosaic glass tiles. Its elaborate design and facilities were created with the sole purpose of giving guests the royal treatment. The hotel also regularly hosts some of the world's finest art exhibitions, such as a Picasso exhibit and a showcase of Islamic and Arabic art.

Hilton Abu Dhabi

www.hilton.com; 02 6811900; Corniche Road, near Marina Mall

If you can't afford to book a room at Emirates Palace but still want to be able to gaze at it, I suggest the Hilton Abu Dhabi, which is kitty corner to Emirates Palace. Choose one of its 350 beautifully decorated rooms and suites and you get access to the fitness center, three tennis courts and spa. Dine at the hotel's Le Terrazza or enjoy fine cuisine at BiCE followed by live music at the Jazz Bar. Vasco's restaurant is a hangout for many VIPs. Abu Dhabi attractions like Marina Mall are just a kilometer away, and the family park is within walking distance.

Shangri-La Hotel

**www.shangri-la.com;
02 509 8888; Bain al Jisran or
Between two bridges**

The Shangri-La Hotel offers an impressive variety of services and facilities, and really is a destination within a destination. You will get a taste of Arabian hospitality when you enter; a man in a kandoura will offer you gahwa (Arabic coffee) and dates. I personally recommend it. There are two pools connected by a series of manmade canals and a beach that faces the Sheikh Zayed Grand Mosque.

The St. Regis Saadiyat Island Resort

www.stregissaadiyatisland.com; 02 498 8888; Saadiyat Island
I could not resist it and had to take my son for his first-ever little holiday there and my family spend a really unforgettable and relaxing weekend. The hotel has something for everybody: Pampering a la carte in the Iridium Spa, Golfing at the 18 hole championship course, designed by Gary Player, Located at one of the Island, chances are good to see even some Hawksbill Turtles and Bottlenose Dolphins.

Beach Rotana Hotel

www.rotana.com; 02 697 9000; next to Abu Dhabi Mall
The Beach Rotana Hotel is one of the hotels I regularly recommend. The moment guests step into the lobby, they are embraced by the unique blend of traditional Arabian hospitality and modern luxury. There are 10 fabulous restaurants; my favorite is Finz, the best seafood restaurant in the city. The hotel is attached to Abu Dhabi Mall, a great venue for shopping and spending some cash.

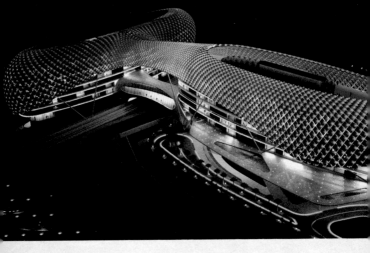

The Yas Hotel
www.theyashotel.com; 02 656 0700; Yas Marina, Yas Island
There is nothing else like this in the Middle East. The hotel's futuristic exterior changes color at night. It overlooks the Formula 1 race track and I can tell you it was quite an experience visiting the site when the track was being built. Finally there is the great service. It is the perfect combination: a hotel that is unique on the outside and delivers such a high standard of service on the inside. Guests, start your engines.

Oryx Hotel
www.oryxhotel.ae; 02 681 0001; Khalidiya Street near Prestige Cars
I love the name of this pretty hotel, which is a reminder of the most beautiful gazelle (referred to as Al Maha). It is located just a short walk from the Corniche and lots of quality shopping. Although small, the Oryx has everything you need. You can unwind in the spa or beside the rooftop swimming pool that has fantastic panoramic views of Abu Dhabi island.

Fairmont Bab Al Bahr

www.fairmont.com/babalbahr; 02 654 3333;
Bain al Jisran or Between two bridges

When driving over the Maqta bridge, you won't miss this hotel because of the building's sleek horizontal lines and design. Like the Shangri-La Hotel, the Fairmont overlooks the Sheikh Zayed Grand Mosque, which is stunning, especially at night when it is lit up. Take in the hotel's famous brunch or grab a burger at its poolside bar.

InterContinental

www.intercontinental.com; 02 666 6888; Al Bateen Area

I have been witness to the renovation of this hotel – it was great before and it's amazing now! It enjoys a prime location on the Arabian Gulf, a few minutes away from the city center and on one of the city's most established harbors, perfect for yacht watching. The trendy international restaurants include Belgian, Brazilian and Italian, and the bountiful Selections buffet.

One to One Hotel – The Village
www.onetoonehotels.com/thevillage; 02 495 2000;
Al Salam Street
Welcome to the neighborhood! This boutique hotel opened right
in the area of my office. The hotel is designed like a village, with its
128 rooms divided into 18 clusters, each with their own rooftop
pool. It features a great outdoor space for eating and drinking and
has play areas for children.

Le Royal Méridien
www.starwoodhotels.com; 02 674 2020; Sheikh Khalifa Street
Home to some of Abu Dhabi's finest restaurants and my expat
friends say the bars and clubs there are fantastic. Al Fanar, the
rotating restaurant at the top of the hotel, has some of the best
views of the city while offering fantastically decadent international
cuisine. They also do a Friday brunch with unlimited champagne
that my friends seem to like. If you fancy a pint of Guinness in the
desert, the Irish pub here seems to draw the crowds, too.

Sheraton Corniche

www.starwoodhotels.com; 02 677 3333; Corniche Road

This hotel has a desert sand feel to it, and features a beautiful view of the Corniche, Abu Dhabi's main walkway along the Arabian Gulf. My friends who have stayed here rave about the beds, which are known to be extra comfy. You can also stay at a Sheraton in the Khalidiya area.

Danat Jebel Dhanna Resort

www.danathotels.com; 02 801 2222;
Jebel Dhanna, Western Region

Picture this: you're lying down in the outdoors, soaking up the sun, sipping fresh juices and just enjoying the moment. OK, now you're probably asking where you could do that? Well, my dear, it's the Danat Jebel Dhanna resort. This getaway is 220km from the city of Abu Dhabi, and is an excellent place to wind down over the weekend.

Desert Islands

www.desertislands.anantara.com; 02 801 5400; Western Region

Located in the Western Region of Abu Dhabi, this wildlife reserve is located on Sir Bani Yas Island. The island is home to thousands of animals and birds, some of which are endangered. It's an ideal destination to experience nature and wildlife, while still enjoying the beauty of the island.

Qasr Al Sarab

www.qasralsarab.anantara.com; 02 886 2088; Western Region

Fancy going for a truly luxurious Arabian getaway? Qasr Al Sarab (pictured at right), the Western Region's best kept secret, is located in the Liwa desert, some 200km away from the city of Abu Dhabi. It features palatial suites and cultural activities such as archery, camel trekking and desert walks. This place is an invitation to the past and into the golden sands of the Empty Quarter. I love going there when I want to get out of the city and relax for a day or two.

For more accommodation options, visit www.ask-ali.com.

Media

An easy and fun way to start learning about the UAE and Arab culture is to switch on the television, listen to the radio or read a newspaper. You might not understand everything that is said, but you will get an idea of body language, dress code and what types of programs we like.

I recommend you start with the TV show *Freej*. Not only is it set in the UAE and created by an Emirati, it's one of the top-rated shows in the Gulf. It was inspired by *The Golden Girls*, which was my favorite program when I studied in the US. The 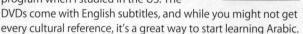 DVDs come with English subtitles, and while you might not get every cultural reference, it's a great way to start learning Arabic.

Also, check out *City of Life*, a recent Emirati film set in Dubai that explores the multicultural fabric of the city's diverse people.

The other DVD I recommend is an animated movie about Allah's messenger called *Muhammad: The Last Prophet*. The movie is an accessible way to familiarize yourself with our religion's origins.

Newspapers

The National

This Abu Dhabi-based newspaper was launched under the patronage of the Crown Prince in April 2008. It has won a number of design awards, and is the most-read English newspaper among Emiratis. It is published seven days a week with daily sections devoted to news, business, sports and arts and life. *The National on Saturday* features the magazine *M*, in which I write a column answering readers' questions about my country's culture.

Gulf News

This Dubai-based daily has been around since 1978 and is the most-read paper in the UAE. Its arts section, *Tabloid*, covers Bollywood like no other. It also has the largest classified section of the major newspapers, as well as the weekly magazine *Friday*.

Khaleej Times

Khaleej means Gulf in Arabic and the *Times* was the first English daily to be launched here way back in 1978. The paper features news, business, sports and a Friday magazine called *wknd*.

7 Days

A local English tabloid publication that is circulated for free in major public outlets in the UAE. Its headlines often make me laugh. That's British humor for you.

Sport 360°

For all the latest news on my beloved Al Jazira football team, I have found this paper gives it proper coverage. *Sport 360°* has amazing photography and treats the world of sports with a mix of serious reporting and a sense of humor.

Emirates 24|7

This online news site provides comprehensive and analytical news coverage for its readers. (www.emirates247.com)

Emarat Al Youm

One of the popular Arabic newspapers that I frequently read is the tabloid-style *Emarat Al Youm*, a very informative, well-designed newspaper focused on local news and events.

TV stations

You can get almost any channel and any English program via satellite so you'll never have to miss a big event again. We also have many regional channels that you probably aren't familiar with that carry English programs. You can purchase channel bundles from Etisalat or Orbit Showtime that offer digital packages, with hundreds of different international and local channels. Some residential complexes may also add their own preferred channels via satellite. Below is the list of local channels we have in the UAE in both English and Arabic.

Abu Dhabi Media Company; www.admedia.ae
A network of English and mostly Arabic programming including the free-to-air National Geographic Abu Dhabi and Al Riyadiya channels – sports stations with a regional (and soccer!) focus. Al Oula channel airs local news and government programs and Al Emarat shows *Inside The National* as well as movies and gameshows.

Dubai Media Incorporated (DMI); www.dmi.ae
Dubai's mother network of all media-related matters. It runs a variety of English and Arabic channels that cater to different viewers and market segments. Channels that fall under DMI are Dubai TV, Sama Dubai, Dubai One, Dubai Sports, Noor Dubai and more.

Dubai One
Dubai's main English channel airing a mix of global entertainment, local talk shows and news. It is hard to get bored with this channel as it always has interesting shows that bridge cultural gaps.

MBC; www.mbc.net

A network of free-to-air English and Arabic stations, broadcasting 24 hours a day from Dubai Media City and available via satellite across the Middle East and North Africa.

MBC 1
An Arabic channel showcasing local and regional Arabic series and entertainment programs.

MBC 2
An English channel focusing on Hollywood movies.

MBC 3
A children's channel that is primarily Arabic with some English programming.

MBC 4
An English channel showing mainly US shows, including shopping and lifestyle.

MBC Max
Similar to MBC 2 – with even more movie premieres.

MBC Action
An English channel airing primarily US action series.

The best of the rest...

Al Arabiya
An Arabic-language news channel.

Al Jazeera
The main news source of the Arab world, broadcast in Arabic and English.

Nojoom1, 2, 3 and 4
Arabic and Emirati music and poetry channels.

Radio

If you turn your radio dial, you will hear many different languages, proving just how multicultural the UAE is. There are stations in Tagalog, Urdu, Hindi, Arabic and English.

This is a great opportunity to check out what the rest of the world is listening to, including Al Emarat and Al Khaleejia FM, which play all our favorite local artists.

Frequency	Station	Content	Language
87.9 MHz	BBC World Service	News	English/ Arabic
90.0 MHz, 98.4 MHz	Abu Dhabi FM (AD)	Talk / classic Arabic hits	Arabic
90.5 MHz	Radio Sawa	Arabic and English top 40	Arabic
92.0 MHz	Dubai 92	Rock / contemporary	English
92.4 MHz, 99.9 MHz	Star FM (AD)	Arabic and English top 40	Arabic
93.9 MHz	Dubai FM	Islamic spiritual	Arabic
94.4 MHz	Sharjah FM	Religious / talk	Arabic
94.7 MHz	Cool FM	Bollywood hits / entertainment	Hindi / Urdu
95.8MHz, 97.1 Mhz	Al Emarat FM (AD)	Arabic / Emirati Hits	Arabic
97.8 MHz	UAQ FM	Arabic classic hits	Arabic
98.1 MHz	Quran Al Kareem (AD)	Quran / religious	Arabic
99.3 MHz, 106.0 MHz	Radio 2	Classic hits	English

Frequency	Station	Content	Language
100.5 MHz, 104.1MHz	Radio 1 (AD)	Top 40 / dance / R&B	English
100.9 MHz	Al Khaleejia	Khaleeji music	Arabic
101.6 MHz	City FM	Contemporary hits	Hindi
103.2 MHz	The Coast	Easy listening	English
103.8 MHz	Dubai Eye	News / talk / sport	English
104.4 MHz	Virgin Radio	Top 40	English
104.8 MHz	Channel 4 FM	Top 40	English
105.4 MHz	Radio Spice	South Asian hits	Hindi, English, Spanish and Tamil
106.2 MHz	Hum FM	Indian classic hits	Hindi / Urdu
107.8 MHz	Al Rabea	Arabic hits	Arabic

Psst...

You might notice that some shopping malls, restaurants or supermarkets turn off their music during the adhaan (call to prayer). They do it as a sign of respect. If you are listening to your car radio when you hear the call, it is appropriate to turn down the volume. Also, if you are having a conversation in public, try not to speak too loudly. It's only two minutes, after all.

Postal services

Emirates Post, the sole provider of postal services in the UAE, has 15 branches in Abu Dhabi that provide domestic, international and courier services. Working hours vary among different offices, with some remaining open until late in the evening and others only until early afternoon. Posting mail within the country only costs 50 fils per item under 20 grams. The same letter costs about Dhs3 to Europe or the US.

Private courier companies such as Aramex, DHL and FedEx provide fast and efficient delivery services between Abu Dhabi and the world, as does Emirates Post's courier subsidiary. Call or visit the following websites to find the closest branch to you:

Emirates Post
600 565 555; www.empostuae.com

Aramex
600 544 000; www.aramex.com

DHL
800 4004; www.dhl.co.ae

FedEx
800 4050; www.fedex.com/ae

Our telecommunications provider, Etisalat, also provides various packages of fast and efficient internet services. As with other forms of media, please be aware that the Internet is monitored by a special department of the Government, which filters out sites that offend our religious and political standards or contain sexual content. If you come across content that you don't think is objectionable, you can contact Etisalat to request that the page be unblocked.

Psst...

The Flickr ban has been lifted in the UAE, so if you're nuts about sharing your photography, you can continue to do so. Just remember not to post sexually suggestive or politically or religiously controversial material.

Social media

Emiratweet

www.emiratweet.com

Want to be kept up to date with everything Emirati from events, news, street talk and prayer times? Emiratweet is the first Emirati online social community (virtual majlis), an initiative to maintain and preserve our national identity by providing information, facts and news about Emirati individuals and society. I urge you to embrace this active social media outlet on Facebook and Twitter, and to get involved in the conversations and events that are organized by Emiratweet.

Psst...

Want to know more about successful entrepreneurial Emiratis? Check out the online Sail magazine at www.sailemagazine.com, where you can learn more about young active Emiratis who are making a difference not only in this part of the world but all over the globe.

Navigating

The capital is quite remarkable, considering what it looked like 20 or even 10 years ago. Beautiful buildings and excellent roads have replaced, well, the desert.

However, when progress moves this quickly, there are bound to be some growing pains. Getting around Abu Dhabi can be frustrating because of road works. Please be patient as we continue our modernization.

Psst...

Here are important words that you will come across while driving. The stop sign in Arabic is قف and exit is مخرج Memorize them – they will come in handy, even though you will find many that are written in English, too. But just in case.

One quirk is that western-style addresses are seldom used; instead we navigate using landmarks. Making it even more difficult is street naming: many of the major roads have more than one name, one of which is often the name of a sheikh. For example, Sheikh Zayed The First Street has four names: Sheikh Zayed The First is its official name; it is also 7th Street, but it is commonly known as Khalidiya to the west of Airport Road and Electra to the east. Confusing, I know, but you'll soon be an expert and think nothing of asking a cab to take your favorite route.

For instance, if you want a taxi to take you to the Cultural Foundation, you would tell your driver to go to Al Hosn Fort or the White Fort, which is also in the area of the Marks & Spencer building. Or you could say Al Mujama al Thaqafi, which is the Arabic name for the foundation.

In general, give directions based first on Government buildings, then hotels, hospitals, major supermarkets and the area (eg. Al Bateen). It's good to have a full vision of how the city is laid out and the important landmarks.

Driving

Welcome to the Arab version of the NASCAR Daytona 500! Here you will find a – how should I put it? – more aggressive driving culture, so you should be aware of the rules of the road.

The speed limit in the city varies from 60-80kph (37-50mph), while highways leading you out of the city are 120kph (75mph). This can differ according to the emirate and road. Be aware that many drivers do not adhere to these limits.

We drive on the right side of the road. At intersections, traffic moves in one direction at a time. U-turns are almost always allowed. Left-hand turns can be made from the middle and left lanes. We have many roundabouts; give way to cars on your left.

Cars are king in our culture. Pedestrians shouldn't assume that cars will stop for them. Some driving habits might be unfamiliar to westerners; we flash our high beams if we want to pass, and lay on our horns to make other drivers aware of our presence. These gestures are not meant to be hostile, so try to keep your cool. Reacting with obscene gestures can land you in jail.

Psst...

Even though you might see lots of people speeding, I recommend you stick to the speed limit. Speed cameras are set up around the city, and the fines for speeding (up to Dhs800) just aren't worth it. You get demerit points on your license if you are breaking the speed limit by a substantial amount. If you are pulled over by the police here, you can politely request them to let you off with a verbal warning. A man can get out of his car, but a woman has the option to stay inside. If you are in an accident stay at the scene until the police get there.

Driver's licenses

International driver's licenses are recommended until you receive your residence visa. If you are lucky enough to be from one of the following countries you can exchange your license for a local one: Australia, Austria, Bahrain, Belgium, Canada, Denmark, Finland, France, Germany, Greece, Ireland, Italy, Japan, South Korea, Kuwait, Netherlands, New Zealand, Norway, Oman, Poland, Qatar, Romania, Saudi Arabia, South Africa, Spain, Sweden, Switzerland, Turkey, United Kingdom, United States.

To get a license you will need to bring the following to the Traffic and Licensing Department of the General Police Directorate on Al Saada Street (02 419 5555):

1. A photocopy of your passport with a copy of your residence visa. Bring the original as well.

2. Three recent passport-size photos. (I told you we like pictures!)

3. Your current valid license, translated into Arabic. Translation fees cost Dhs110 or less for an urgent application, which takes 24 hours.

4. A no-objection letter from your sponsor if you are here on a family visa.

5. Dhs200 for the application fee.

If you are not from one of the countries listed above, you must take a driving test. The Abu Dhabi Police have an application form online (www.adpolice.gov.ae/en) under Services or you can contact the Emirates Driving Company (02 551 1911) for more information.

Your driving experience will dictate how long it takes to get your license from a driving center, as well as how much it costs. If you are learning from scratch, for example, it will take longer and cost more than if you have transferred from another country and just need a few hours with a trainer to get accustomed to Abu Dhabi's roads.

For contacts of legal translation offices, visit www.ask-ali.com.

Buying a car

Another reason the car is king in the UAE is because cars cost less here, sometimes as much as 30 per cent cheaper than in the West. Most of the makes that you are familiar with – Mercedes-Benz, Porsche, Mini, BMW, Volkswagen, Nissan – are available here.

To buy a car in the UAE, you must have a residence visa. You will also need your passport to register your new baby through the Abu Dhabi Police. If you buy from a dealership, they will often do much of the paperwork for you.

If you are buying a used car, here are some important things to be aware of:
1. Dealerships often charge more for second-hand cars than private sales, but they usually offer a warranty and a service workshop.

Psst...

We care a lot about cars; in fact, a recent study showed that Emirati poets are now writing more about automobiles and less about camels. I find that hard to comprehend. Part of our dedication is making sure our cars are clean. You'll see we even cover our seats with plastic to keep the interiors spotless. Technically, it is illegal to wash your car in public, but many apartment watchmen will clean your car once a week if you slip them Dhs50-Dhs100 each month. If you want that new-car look, take a trip out to Mussafah City, an industrial area 20 minutes outside of Abu Dhabi where you will find many shops that polish, clean, tint and sell add-ons for your precious baby. Some people paint the bottom of the chassis body with a muddy sandy color as a way to protect their car from any scratches caused by rocks and other debris.

Also...

You will notice the majority of car windows are tinted; this is for 2 reasons. Tinting helps reduce heat from the intense summer sun, and also helps maintain privacy, especially for women. Tinting shops can be found on Salam Street; even malls offer one-hour tinting services near their parking lots. FYI: The maximum legal tinting percentage is 30 per cent.

2. An inspection from a good mechanic costs about Dhs300, but it is a good idea with used cars. Make sure to book in advance.

3. There is usually some room for haggling when buying either a new or used car.

4. When registering a used car in your name, you must transfer ownership. Once you get the transfer application from the Abu Dhabi Traffic Police, you will also need an NOC (no objection certificate) letter from the bank if you financed the car, the original plates, the valid registration card, insurance certificate and Dhs20. The former owner also needs to be present to sign the form.

Parking

Abu Dhabi was built for half the number of people who live here now. One of the consequences of this quick development is the lack of parking. Mawaqif is a new paid parking initiative that was introduced last year to ease congestion, and trust me, it worked wonders in  many areas. Slots marked in blue and black, or blue and white, are paid parking zones. So either make sure you have enough coins, or buy the pre-paid Mawaqif card available in supermarkets. I highly recommend that you register with Mawaqif if you live in a paid parking area. It's cheaper than paying every day and less of a hassle. (www.mawaqif.ae)

Psst...

You won't have to resort to this too often, but if you double park out of emergency, then leave a piece of paper on the windshield with your mobile phone number on it. Then, if someone needs to get out, they can call you. You see this all the time. Or if it's you who is blocked in and a cellphone number has not been left, call 999 and give them the car's license plate number and color, and they will call the owner.

Gas stations

Psst...

You will notice the gentleman filling your petrol will also come to you and wave his hands. Don't wave back because he is not saying hello, rather he is asking if you would like your windshield cleaned. This is a free service by ADNOC as they like to go above and beyond their customers' expectations. It is up to you if you want to tip them for cleaning your windshield.

In Abu Dhabi there is no need to get out of your car when you drive into a gas station, because there is an army of blue-suited employees to pump your gas and clean your windshield for you.

ADNOC (Abu Dhabi National Oil Company) has introduced self-service pumps to appeal to expats, but you rarely see anyone use them. One of the advantages of living here is the service-oriented culture, so there is no need to leave your car. Our gas stations also include a convenience store brand called Oasis, a refreshment area for tea, coffee and light snacks, not to mention one or two restaurants to feed your growling tummy.

Taxis

If you want to avoid the hassle of driving, taxis are an inexpensive alternative. Silver cabs always have seat belts and use the meter. Gold and white taxis are being phased out, but if you do get one, be warned: drivers tend to try to negotiate with you, especially at night. To go anywhere on Abu Dhabi island, the fare shouldn't be more than Dhs30. You can call 600 535353 to book a taxi with TransAd. Their service is efficient; once you book, you will be sent an SMS of the license plate number of the taxi picking you up, the name of the driver and how long it will take them to reach you.

Tipping

You are not obliged to tip, but in our Arabic culture we are used to giving money as a show of ikramiya (generosity) to those who do a good job or just try their best.

You need not tip someone every time you see them. For example, tip your regular valet once at the beginning or at the end of the month, not every time he parks your car.

Tipping is not expected and therefore it does not matter if the amount is Dhs5 or Dhs500, as long as the intention is generosity, which is highly valued here.

You will also notice that your bill at many hotel restaurants includes a service charge. This does not necessarily go to the hotel staff, so if you want to show your appreciation for the service you received, you should do so in cash.

uses

The Government introduced public buses in 2008 to ease traffic congestion. They were originally free of charge, but now cost Dh1. This is a cheap, hassle-free way to get around the city. There are about a dozen routes covering the island end-to-end – from Marina Mall to Abu Dhabi Mall and Sheikh Zayed mosque. Make sure you either study the route maps or pay attention to the destination on the front of the bus. The Abu Dhabi Central Bus Station is on Muroor Road.

You can take buses to all the emirates, although taxis take a lot less time and it could be more cost-effective if there are a few of you to share the price.

Health care

You'll find leading clinics staffed with excellent doctors and other medical professionals from a variety of countries in Abu Dhabi. There are options to suit all budgets and cultural expectations. Many medications are available over the counter at the pharmacy and most major pharmacies are open 24 hours. Here are a few of Abu Dhabi's best-known hospitals.

Sheikh Khalifa Medical City
www.skmc.ae; 02 819 0000;
Between Airport Road and Karama Street
The famous Cleveland Clinic partnered with this hospital and manages it today. Almost 4,000 staff are employed in this multi-disciplinary facility, which includes a dentistry unit, a blood bank and a diabetes center. It also has a surgical pavilion and a behavioral science center.

Al Noor Hospital
www.alnoorhospital.com; 02 444 66 55; Airport Road
This hospital is a calm respite from the noise of the city and, with its nearby garden, is a great place to convalesce. Al Noor has the most up-to-date technologies, including surgical theaters for spinal, orthopedic and cardiac operations.

Gulf Diagnostic Center
www.gdc-hospital.com; 02 665 8090; Khaleej Al Arabi Street
This is a favorite among the local and expat community. It has a vast array of specialist departments from psychiatric to cardiology, with up-to-date testing facilities and equipment. They regularly liaise with their international counterparts.

New Medical Centre

www.nmc.ae; 02 633 2255; Electra Street, Madinat Zayed

Over 100 doctors and 400 paramedics work at the first multi-disciplinary hospital in Abu Dhabi. The radiology department is the largest in the city, and the hospital is a good place to go if you aren't sure if and where you will need to be referred. They also have an in-house pharmacy for your convenience.

Dar Al Shifa Hospital

www.daralshifa.net; 02 641 6999; Defense Road

Dar Al Shifa means "house of healing". This hospital is quite popular with the locals as their facilities and services are extensive, so it would be a good idea to make an appointment and save time.

Corniche Hospital

www.cornichehospital.ae; 02 672 4900; near Sheraton Hotel

If you were born in Abu Dhabi, chances are your mom delivered you at Corniche Hospital. This has been Abu Dhabi's leading hospital for the past 25 years in gynecology and obstetrics.

Traditional medical centers

Moving to an Islamic country is the perfect opportunity for you to try some of our traditional medical techniques such as hijama. Practitioners make tiny incisions in the skin then use negative pressure to suck out toxic blood. Hijama is an example of following what the Prophet Mohammed (PBUH) recommended, and is used to treat many maladies, especially aches and pains.

Try Al Rahma Medical Center on Hamdan Street (02 676 7171).

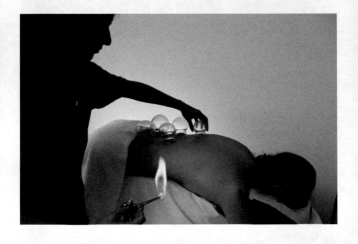

Gulf Chinese Medical Centre

02 634 3538; Airport Road and Hamdan Street

Traditional Arab medicine is based on a very similar, meridian-based philosophy to Chinese medicine. Dr Hu Qiwen has practiced Chinese medicine for many years and was certified in the United States to practice acupuncture, which has been proven effective in treating certain conditions such as arthritis. The staff are also versed in massage, cupping therapy and traditional Chinese herbs.

Chiropractic Specialty Clinics of the Emirate

www.chiropracticuae.com; 02 634 5162

As many of us spend more and more time sitting at our desks, our backs are taking the strain. Chiropractic care can be a useful tool in relieving lower back and neck pain and maintaining proper posture. The practitioners at CSC (one male, one female) use adjustments, massage and electro-stimulation to bring normal function back to the spine. They can also be used as consultants when it comes to setting up the proper ergonomic work environment.

Dentists

Dentistry is seldom fully covered by your company's health insurance provider. So make sure you investigate prices from different clinics before agreeing to a procedure. Most clinics associate themselves with the country the dentist came from, ie. American, British, Swedish. The Gulf Diagnostic Center also has a dentistry clinic. Cosmetic dentistry is not usually covered by insurance at all.

Manners

Settling down in a new country not only means learning where everything is, but also entails gaining a better understanding of our culture. As part of my mission as your friendly cultural guide, I have come up with these 19 suggestions. Remember them and locals will always appreciate it.

1. You might see Gulf men greet each other by rubbing noses; this is specific to the region, so expats need not worry about doing it. Instead, try saying Marhaba or As salamu alaykum (see page 230).

2. Men shake hands with men and women shake hands with women. Shake firmly. If you are a man, it is impolite to offer your hand to a local woman. If they offer their hand, it is OK to reciprocate. Some Arab men will shake western women's hands, but please don't be offended if we don't.

3. Be patient. It takes time to network, which is the most important thing you can do. Emiratis prefer to build a friendship first and then build a business relationship.

4. Saving face is important. Even if you must compromise, don't embarrass your Arab colleagues in public. It might end up embarrassing you. This doesn't mean being dishonest, it just means being thoughtful.

5. Verbal agreements are very important. Try to keep your business dealings confidential to honor the other person's trust in you.

6. We have a more relaxed attitude when it comes to business culture, so you can be more relaxed, too. Please be patient and try to remember that our priorities are sometimes different from other cultures.

7. We consider business associates more like friends, so if we have an urgent family matter or business dealing, we hope you will understand if we walk out of a meeting. We mean no disrespect and won't be upset if you do the same.

8. Some Arabs might answer their cellphones during meetings. Some of us consider it disrespectful not to answer a call, as opposed to western culture where the opposite is true.

9. Good conversation starters include enquiring after the health of a person and their family. Or sports, especially soccer.

10. Arabs love to host. We are most comfortable at home so when you are invited for a meal, try to accept. It is the best way to learn about our culture.

11. If you are invited to an Emirati's home, the family often eats sitting on the floor, so wear something comfortable and modest.

12. Follow your host regarding etiquette. They might remove their shoes before entering the majlis, (the Arab living room), so you should do the same.

13. When it comes to an authentic cup of gahwa (coffee), shake your cup if you don't want any more. Accept the cup with your right hand (see number 17).

14. Arabic sweets are delicious so make sure you don't leave until after coffee and dessert are served. If you leave prior to this, your hosts may feel they have not completed their hospitality duties.

15. Don't point the bottom of your feet towards an Arab's face. Come to think of it, don't show the soles of your feet to anyone.

16. We tend to be close talkers and use a lot of body language when we speak. We often touch the other person (same sex only). We might raise our voices, not out of anger, but to emphasize a point.

17. Use your right hand to pick things up or accept things. The left hand was once used for hygienic purposes and while this is no longer the custom, it is still thought of as unclean. Don't worry if you are left-handed. The US President Barack Obama is a leftie, and he is still very popular here.

18. When standing with others at an elevator or at a doorway, we allow the person on our right to go in first. Yamin means right, but you can also use it to indicate that the other person may go first. We may even reshuffle our position to place a distinguished guest to our right. When we host a business meeting, we make sure that the guest of honor is seated to our right.

19. Modesty and respect are the Arab world's greatest virtues. Please use these as a guideline for everything from dress code to business behavior.

Socializing tips

The smallest gesture can so often be the most important. Get it wrong and it's always embarrassing. Who would want to unwittingly insult someone just because they were unaware of a way of doing things that was different to what they were used to?

We like to communicate face-to-face and that, of course, means you can see what the other person is doing. So here are some clear steps to avoid insult, even if it's the last thing you would want to do:

When you…	It comes across as…
Don't stand up when someone approaches you to say hello	Being impolite, especially if the person approaching you is older than you or has a high position or status
Don't say Mashallah when praising something beautiful to an Arab	Being envious and not blessing what you are praising
Choose to say Persian Gulf instead of Arabian Gulf	Not appreciating the Arab Gulf region
Invite someone for a drink, knowing he is a devout Muslim	Being disrespectful, as most Muslims don't drink. If they do, they prefer not to be invited so as to protect their reputation
Don't say PBUH (if you are a Muslim) after mentioning any of the prophets	Unappreciative and disregarding the prophet's greatness
Touch or slowly pat the shoulder or the behind of the opposite sex	Misbehaving or hinting to something sexual, which could raise questions about your relationship with that person
Use a lot of swear words repeatedly	Being impolite and unpleasant to be around

Call to prayer

One of the five central pillars of our religion is praying each day. But we don't just pray once a day; we do it five times. And, no, it's not to get out of work! To remind us that it's time to pray, the muaadhin (prayer caller) from the mosque will call out through loudspeakers. These men are not only dedicated to Islam, they have beautiful voices, which can soothe the minds of even non-Muslim listeners. Since prayers are so important to us, you will notice that all shopping malls and commercial buildings have prayer rooms and ablution washrooms.

Psst...

When the first prayer of the day (fajr) is called at the break of dawn, the muaadhin also adds a small phrase that says "Assalatu khayrun minan nauum" which means "Prayer is better than sleeping". This is a reminder to the faithful that it's time to get up and pray.

Mosques

The Arabic word for mosque is masjid. There are mosques in every neighborhood so there is no excuse for us to miss prayers. Islam strives to accommodate every devotee, so if you are Muslim and are used to English-speaking imams (religious teachers), you won't have to miss Jumaa prayer. There is a mosque in Al Bateen (32nd Street, near Oriental Spa) that offers prayers in English. There are also translations in Urdu. Contact the Abu Dhabi Judicial Department, Embracing Islam division (02 444 8300) for information.

Log on to the Islamic General Authority of Islamic Affairs & Endowment at www.awqaf.ae or call 800 2422 for spiritual advice. They offer useful services such as speaking with a Sheikh. A Sheikh (see page 241) is a religious scholar and can give you on-the-spot counseling and guidance for any problems concerning your life and Islam.

You do not have to be Muslim to speak to a Sheikh. They welcome calls from people of all religions with an open heart, and they keep information confidential. There are Sheikhs who speak Arabic, English, Urdu, Hindi, French, Russian and Persian.

For those who are seeking to learn more about Islam, the General Authority of Islamic Affairs & Endowment also conducts workshops and seminars – you can even download the Friday sermons from their website.

Jumaa means "gathering", which is appropriate since we all gather as families on Fridays. It's a time for the elderly to sit, talk, learn and laugh with younger generations, which we believe is important for family bonding. On Fridays, we also thank Allah for the blessings and guidance of the past week and ask that He bless us for the week to come. I'm positive that many of us men wait impatiently for this day to have their mom's cooking, especially dishes like machboos hammour (our local fish and rice pilaf dish).

Psst...

Now that you know Friday is our resting day, I suggest that you do not schedule meetings or sports on a Friday, at least not until after 4pm. Anytime before that is dedicated to prayers and spending time with family.

Churches

We invite our Christian brothers and sisters to worship in Abu Dhabi. You can find all the churches listed below located in the same area in the city: near the Immigration Department, just off Airport Road, near Karamah Street.

Arabic Evangelical Church
www.eccad.org; 02 443 4350

Evangelical Community Church
www.eccad.org; 02 446 4563

Saint Andrews Church
(Anglican, Episcopal)
www.standrewauh.org; 02 446 1631

Indian Evangelical Church
www.eccad.org; 02 446 3043

Saint George Orthodox Church
www.indianorthodoxchurchabudhabi.com;
02 446 4564

Saint Joseph's Catholic Church
www.stjosephsabudhabi.org;
02 446 1929

Photography etiquette

We want you to keep pleasant memories of our country, so please take photographs. However, you should ask permission if you want to photograph a local person (women and families in particular). Most people will be happy to pose for a photograph if you have their approval first.

You might walk by a mosque in your neighborhood and naturally want to snap some pictures. As a matter of respect, we ask people not to photograph Muslims who are praying because it could distract them from their worship. Taking pictures of military sites or the royal family's palaces is also not advisable and you'll see signs warning against doing so. In fact, this goes for any Government building including airports and police headquarters.

It is easy to get swept up in how photogenic Abu Dhabi can be, but try to be aware of our sensitivities, your surroundings and what's appropriate to photograph.

Ramadan

The holy month of Ramadan is the ninth month of the Islamic lunar calendar. Every day during this month, Muslims abstain from food and drink during daylight hours. The fast is intended to purify the body, but Ramadan is also a time for purification of the mind and spirit through increased prayer. Children usually begin fasting at the age of seven, although only for half the day at first. The sick, elderly or those who are traveling do not need to fast, but should make up for it with increased prayer or charity.

A typical Ramadan night starts with a call to the evening (maghrib) prayer, which signifies the breaking of the sawm (fast).

The fast is usually broken with a date and a cup of yogurt. The maghrib prayer is followed by iftar or futoor (these words are interchangeable in the UAE and translate as breakfast): a meal of harees, thareed and green salad are popular dishes.

Iftar is followed by the ishaa or evening prayer. Muslims can also do a taraweeh (comforting) prayer, to soothe the body and mind after a hard day of fasting. The change in eating habits alters the biological clock and during Ramadan most socializing takes place in the evening. Many sporting and cultural events are held at this time, often not winding down until the early hours.

Before the sun comes up followers wake for suhoor, which is a light meal, ideally without meat, consisting of leftovers from iftar and pita bread. There is a short period known as imsak, in which we stop eating, then we engage in the fajr (dawn) prayer.

During Ramadan, working hours change to accommodate fasting Muslims. Usually, offices and shops will open two hours later and close two hours earlier, while many restaurants and coffee shops will remain closed until iftar.

The end of Ramadan is the most religious period, with followers often spending more time at the mosque or even visiting Mecca (Makkah). The last 10 days include Laylat Al Qadr, or the Night of Power, which is the night the holy Quran was revealed to Prophet Mohammed (PBUH). The holy month ends with Eid Al Fitr, which is a time of great socializing. There is a charming tradition in which parents, older siblings and family friends give money and gifts to young children and share food with their neighbors.

Psst...

Another way to get involved with Ramadan is to join the Ask Ali iftar programs. Learn about the meaning of Ramadan and break the fast with us in an Emirati-style majlis. For more details e-mail info@embracearabia.com

Considerations during Ramadan

It is nice for non-Muslims to show support for their Muslim friends and neighbors. As a sign of respect, it is advisable not to eat, drink, smoke or chew gum in public, except in designated areas in offices and hotels. You might even try fasting to experience what Muslims go through during this holy month.

At the beginning of the month, feel free to send a Ramadan Kareem (which means "Blessed Ramadan") card to your Muslim friends, or an Eid Mubarak (which means "Happy Eid") card at the end. A good way to experience the nightlife of Ramadan is to visit the hospitality tents set up around the city, especially at hotels. This is also a good way to network and to try some delicious Arabic food.

You should consider driving more carefully, especially before sunset, around 6pm, at the end of the work day when Muslims are rushing to get home in time for iftar.

It's best to wait until after Ramadan to approach Muslim businessmen with new ideas. If you don't, be aware that their minds will be focused on purification, so allow extra time for answers.

Bars in hotels do not open until iftar and many won't play any music.

Psst...

On the last day of Ramadan or during Eid celebrations you might hear strange explosions. Don't worry, it's just "shellag", fireworks that children set off to celebrate the arrival of Eid.

Handy phrases

Mabrook (congratulations) on taking the first step! Now that you're more comfortable here, try learning some more Arabic. You could also consider taking a course at Berlitz (www.berlitz.ae; 02 667 2287), or The Mother Tongue Arabic Language Centre (www.mothertongue.ae; 02 639 3838)

It is always important to ask yourself why you want to learn Arabic. If it is for work, where a lot of technical jargon is used, you might want to learn classical Arabic. If you just want to learn enough to communicate with the people in your neighborhood, you might prefer to learn the local Khaleeji dialect.

For now, these are some more handy phrases:

Peace be upon you	As salamu alaykum (this phrase is short for As salamu alaykum wa ra hamatu allahi wa baraktuh).
Response	Wa alaykum as salam
Hello	Marhaba
Response	Ya Marhaba / Ahlen
How are you?	(Kaif or Chaif) el hal
I'm well, thanks be to God	Bekhair alhamdulillah
Good morning	Sabahul khair
Response	Sabah al Noor (bright morning)
Good evening	Masaul khair
Response	Masa an noor (bright evening)
Good night	Tesbah ala khair (M)
	Tesbaheen ala khair (F)

Want to learn more? Check out the Arabic phrases on page 230.

Psst...

One of the most common expressions in Arabic is inshallah, which means "If God wills it" or "God willing". In Islam, we believe that everything is in the hands of God, so when we say inshallah, we mean we hope something happens, but it will only happen if God wills it. A lot of expats take inshallah to mean we are absolving ourselves of all responsibility and perhaps seeking an excuse for when things don't turn out as expected. But inshallah is not about results. We simply mean to communicate to God: "This is what I plan to execute, but I cannot do it without your grace." It is about acknowledging God's existence in everything we do or plan to do.

Also...

Let's say you are walking in the mall and spot an Emirati friend or colleague from afar. If you want to impress them, call them by their kunya, or what Arabs call a nickname. Arab men are either referred to as the father of their children, or to nicknames linked to their own name that date back to influential Islamic figures, such as the companions of the Prophet Mohammed (PBUH). Some examples are:

Mohammed is called Abu Jasem, and Jasem called Abu Mohammed in reverse. Abu means "father of", but don't worry, he doesn't have to be a father to get the name – it's just how our nicknames work. My nickname, for example, is "Abu Hasan" and if I meet a man named Hasan, I'll call him "Abu Ali". Also, Yousif is Abu Yaqoub, Khalid is Abu Waleed, and Abdulla is Abu Shihab. For more, check out www.ask-ali.com.

Housing

Construction abounds in Abu Dhabi. We are trying hard to meet the demand for all the people who want to move to our exciting city.

Landlords usually ask for a full year's rent in advance, or in various installments, but some employers will pay this for you and then deduct it from your monthly salary.

Be careful not to get involved with an illegally converted villa because the Government is cracking down on them. A good way to judge if everything is above board is whether the apartment has its own electricity meter.

Rents are highest in the center of the city, with the most desirable addresses downtown near the Corniche, the road that runs along the water, where the view is amazing. Many of the more expensive villas are located in the island's western suburbs. The central part of Abu Dhabi is a good family area, with lots of schools and villas. A new suburb between the city's two bridges is rising in popularity with more modern villas available. More economical options are available outside the city in Mushrif, Musaffah and Shahama. On the edge of town are Al Raha Beach and Khalifa City A developments, where villas often feature swimming pools and garden areas. Mohammed bin Zayed City and Khalifa City A also offer a lot of spacious, affordable homes.

If you are looking to purchase a place, our laws were recently amended to allow foreign ownership and partial ownership on nearby islands such as Al Reem and Saadiyat.

Psst...

City life is very convenient. The common culture in many areas is for pharmacies, grocery and other stores to occupy the ground floor of a building, offices on the mezzanine and accommodation above. Be sure to forge relationships with the shops around your place; go to the grocery the first few times, then open an account. If you live on the 20th floor, for example, you won't have to trudge down every time you want a loaf of bread. Once you open a hisab (account), all you have to do is pop down once a month to pay your bill.

Domestic help

If you decide to employ a maid, there are plenty of agencies that can help you. Just be aware that your domestic help must have a sponsor. Some people hire part-time cleaners, which is illegal if they are not sponsored for that type of work. It's not for me to say whether that person is a "friend", as some people claim, but it can get you into trouble. The Government adopted these regulations to protect both maids and the families they work for from abuse and exploitation. Not only that, an unregistered maid's employer can face charges for hiring illegal help. There are a couple of reputable agencies that can help you find a maid, either full or part time. You can find maid agency contacts in some of the classified newspapers or in the city as you walk by some random advertisements. Call the Abu Dhabi Chamber of Commerce (02 621 4000) for a list of maid agencies. Or, if you want to hire a maid from overseas, I would suggest you visit the immigration department and ask them for an updated regulation guide for hiring new maids. The phone number for the immigration office in Abu Dhabi is 600 522222.

Psst...

When dealing with an agent to hire domestic help from abroad, you may be given a list of portfolios with the résumés of the applicants. Be very specific with what you want; for example, the most important thing may be hiring someone who knows how to speak English if you are an English speaker. You may also call and speak to the maid via the agent to chit chat with her before you decide to hire her.

Furnishing your apartment

The first difference you might notice between renting and owning a house is that apartments here are not usually fitted with appliances. Don't worry – there are plenty of places selling just what you need to fit most budgets.

The hypermarkets – Carrefour and Lulu – carry everything from TVs and ovens to daily grocery items. They will deliver and install any appliances you buy for a minimal charge. They only ask that you draw them a rudimentary map to your home. There is also a gigantic IKEA store on Yas Island. They will deliver and assemble any purchases over Dhs2,000.

We have all types of furniture stores, from high-end luxury to second-hand (if you're really adventurous, try furnishing your whole villa from pieces bought in the Tanker Mai area, or from second-hand stores such as Nefertiti in Al Khalidiya, (www.useditemsuae.com). There are many small lighting and curtain shops in every district. Because of the competition, they usually offer good rates.

Your neighbors

When I was a little boy living on Hamdan Street, I remember being introduced to foods like shawarma and fatoush through our Arab neighbors. My point is that if an Emirati can learn about other cultures in his hometown, you can too. Ask your neighbors about the landmarks in your area or where the local laundry is – anything to get on good terms with those you live close to. It's strange, but expats in the same location can have different attitudes toward their neighborhoods, and this is mostly because of the approach they took when they first moved in.

Groceries

Welcome to the land of foodstuffs. It seems every second baqalla (neighborhood grocer) in Abu Dhabi uses foodstuff in their title. Many of the baqallas will deliver to your home, so make sure to get on good terms with them; you never know when you will need an emergency roll of toilet paper. You will find all your daily supplies at these stores, although you should look to the major supermarkets for fresh produce. There are also convenience stores called dukan, which are smaller and sell more snack items.

Places such as Lulu or Carrefour are called hypermarkets because they stock everything from food to electrical appliances. Spinneys carries many products from the high-end British brand, Waitrose. Besides the staples, Abela also carries Korean and Japanese foods. For great produce, try Mina Port. It's the closest thing we have to a farmers market and also has a wonderful fish market where you can buy the famous Gulf hammour, similar to grouper. As a multicultural city, there are many food influences. You might not be able to purchase all the brands you know, but part of the joy of moving is trying new things. (I will touch on local cuisine later.)

The first Co-op opened in 1981. Now there are more than 10, offering everything from food to electronics with both imported brands and their own house brand. Most of the Co-op stores are known for their everyday discounts and special offers.

The supermarkets listed below have different prices and product ranges, so examine your options first before buying.

Abela
(02 667 4675; Al Khalidiya)
(02 5567061; Etihad Plaza)

Abu Dhabi Co-operative Society
(02 645 9777; Abu Dhabi Mall)
(02 666 4600; Al Bateen Mall)

Spinneys
(02 681 2356; Al Khalidiya)

Carrefour Hypermarket
(02 681 7100; Marina Mall)
(02 449 4300; Airport Road, near Al Futtaim Motors)

Lulu Hypermarket
(02 635 4100; Khalidiya Mall)
(02 443 7500; Al Wahda Mall)

Psst...

In Arabic, we commonly call the store "Al Jami'iya", so even if you're going in a cab, just state which Jami'iya branch you want to go to and he will understand.

Also...

Most residents don't know this, but it is cheaper to buy your veggies and fruits from the market in Madinat Zayed (next to the post office), rather than supermarkets. Not to mention you have the added benefit of bargaining!

Organic food

Major grocers are stocking more and more organic products, and some even have entire aisles dedicated to food produced without chemicals. Abu Dhabi also initiated the country's first organic farm so that residents can think global and eat local. We are also starting to see more restaurants catering to healthy eating choices. A couple that deliver are:

Eat Smart Cafe
02 634 6624; Marks & Spencer building
Eat Smart has an excellent healthy juice selection, as well as lots of yummy salads and buckwheat crepes. Eat Smart also has its own organic grocery store just above the restaurant.

BiteRite Cafe
02 641 1660; New Medical Centre
This restaurant is so devoted to offering low-fat food that they consult nutritionists and endocrinologists for its menu. It offers dishes to suit almost any palate, including Arabic, South Asian, and Indian. They must be healthy, if the hospital allows the cafe to feed its patients! There is also a BiteRite across from the bus station, near the Red Crescent building on Muroor Road.

Psst...

Organic Foods & Cafe supermarket (02 557 1406) has finally come to Abu Dhabi with the recent branch opening in Masdar City. But if you don't feel like making the trip out there, you can order online and pay cash on delivery. Visit their website on www.organicfoodsandcafe.com.

Water

Though our tap water is drinkable, most of us drink bottled water. Depending on your preference, bottled water can be bought for as little as Dh1 or as much as Dhs8. Local water companies such as Masafi and Al Ain share the market with global brands such as Evian and San Pellegrino. When you dine out make sure to ask your waiter for local bottled water if you don't want to pay for the imported stuff. Using tap water for cooking purposes, or making a cup of tea, is absolutely fine.

Liquor licenses

One neat thing many non-Muslim expats find about living here is that you get a license to buy alcohol. It's like having a passport to drink. Each time you purchase liquor, the store will note the date and how much you purchased on your license. The amount you are allowed to purchase is 20 per cent of your monthly salary, but you can only get a license if you earn more than Dhs3,000 a month. Application forms are available at liquor stores and should be returned to the Police Directorate. Visitors cannot buy alcohol from these shops, but can purchase up to four liters duty free at the airport and buy drinks in hotel bars.

Electricity

Owing to our British ties, we use a three-prong plug and 220/240-volt supply with 50Hz. Adapters are easy to find in local shops.

Utilities

I have some bad news for you: you still have to pay bills in Abu Dhabi. For water and electricity, payments can be made at Abu Dhabi Distribution Company customer service centers (a list of which can be found on their website: www.addc.ae). Most major banks either allow you to pay your ADDC bill there or offer a direct transfer facility through online banking. You can also do things the old-fashioned way, by mailing a check.

You can pay your Etisalat and du bills by mail, the bank, direct debit, auto-payment or at drop boxes around the city. In fact, Etisalat has even installed special machines in malls and other shops where you can pay your bills directly.

Laundry and dry cleaning

If you don't have a lot of space in your apartment, you really don't need a washing machine and dryer.

In Abu Dhabi there is an array of laundry services in every neighborhood. We call them maghsala or masbagha. They will come to your front door to pick up your dirty clothes, clean them and bring them back, for a low price. As a precaution, you should find out if your local cleaner has the technology to clean fine fabrics such as silk.

Psst...

Some cleaners mark your clothes discreetly with a felt pen, so make sure to tell them in advance if you don't want them to. You should also specify if you want your shirts hung or folded and whether or not you want them starched.

Some of these laundries will also wash or clean blankets, pillows, bed covers, and some might even do carpets.

Environment

Our recycling laws are developing and environmental awareness is growing across the country. The Government has launched major recycling campaigns in order to educate people about waste. With plastic bags, grocery stores such as Carrefour and Spinneys encourage customers to bring their own bags or buy reusable, eco-friendly cloth bags.

Psst...

In our malls, you'll find workers offering to wash your car while you shop. It is environmentally friendly because it consumes less water and does not leave foam, dirt or water running on the floor.

Visit the Ministry of Environment and Water's website at www.moew.gov.ae for updates on how you can take part in future initiatives to work together to reduce waste.

If you have electronic items you no longer need, you can take them to Plug-Ins in Marina Mall and they will recycle them.

Alternatively, there are ways where you can earn some cash for recycling your mobile phones. Visit www.cashformobiles.me for more details.

Psst...

Bu Tinah's is the region's first and largest UNESCO designated marine biosphere reserve. It houses flamingos, rare hawksbill turtles, dolphins and the planet's second-largest population of dugongs, a large marine mammal that is globally endangered. Bu Tinah is one of the official finalists to be named among the New 7 Wonders of Nature. If you haven't voted for it, I urge you to read up on it and vote by texting Bu Tinah to the number 3888 or through the website: www.butinah.ae.

Beauty salons

It might surprise you to learn that hairstyles are very important to Emirati women. Even though they wear the sheila, when they take it off they want to look their best.

There are salons all over town, so if you want a recommendation then ask someone in your neighborhood. Most salons are located on the ground floor of apartment buildings. The windows are tinted so that no man ever sees the mysteries inside.

Tips and Toes
www.tipsntoeshaven.com; 02 681 8386; Marina Mall
A nail salon for all those mani-pedi lovers. I strongly suggest you book an appointment as it's one of the busiest nail salons in Abu Dhabi.

Sisters Beauty Lounge
www.sistersbeautylounge.com; 02 222 2501; 28th Street, opposite Family Development Foundation
This salon also appears to be a favorite amongst the ladies for its extensive one-stop-shop services when it comes to your beauty needs. Hair treatments, styling, nails, massage, facials and much more. Gosh, I thank God that men do not need to be that high maintenance. All we need is a haircut and shave, and we are in tip-top shape. Jealous?

Psst...
If you live in the area of Khalifa or Mohammed Bin Zayed City, you don't have to go all the way to the city for a manicure; Tips and Toes has a branch in Khalifa City A.

Male grooming

For men, grooming is similar to elsewhere in the world. There are many establishments that offer cuts and shaves. But there is one oddity: we call them saloons instead of salons or barbershops. But rest assured, the only difference inside is that much of the conversation is in Urdu. There's usually no need to chat, though, as most saloons have a TV. Abu Dhabi has also seen a growing trend of saloons that specialize in male grooming. At these places, you can get everything from a haircut and shave to facial treatments, manicures and pedicures

(you gotta have good-looking toes if you're going to wear sandals every day) and even massages. Depending on the haircut, costs range from Dhs20-Dhs100 and a beard trim from Dhs15-Dhs50, but the stylists are all very skilled because they are used to dealing with Emiratis and we sure are demanding customers.

Psst...

Beards are special to Emiratis. You will rarely see a clean-shaven man; at the very least he will keep his mustache. A trip to the barber is part of Gulf culture and you will see some creative facial hair while you are here. Personally, I prefer the razor cut, in which the lines of sideburns, neck and under the bottom lip are clearly defined. The Prophet Mohammed (PBUH) had a beard and many Muslims try to follow his example, but a beard isn't mandatory.

Out and about

Out and about

Contents

Out and about

Attractions

Whether you are visiting or live in Abu Dhabi, you will be spoiled for choice with attractions to see and places to visit. From cultural hot spots to chilled-out venues, your time will be filled with attractions to conquer.

Cultural Foundation and Qasr Al Hosn
www.adach.ae/en; 02 621 5300; Al Mujama al Thaqafi

Although it houses the offices for the Abu Dhabi Authority for Culture and Heritage (ADACH), this building also serves as a *de facto* museum. Inside are artifacts and some of the best art the country has to offer. See a diorama of the city in the 1960s on the top floor. Next to the coffee shop, local women make handicrafts that you can buy. The foundation regularly hosts film nights and lectures. A schedule is available at the front desk.

The place that many call the White Fort is temporarily closed as it is currently being turned into a museum, as part of an attempt to have it registered with UNESCO as a world heritage site. Located next to the Cultural Foundation, it was originally a watchtower built to defend the island's only freshwater well, discovered around 1761 by locals following a herd of gazelles.

Psst...

ADACH holds many exhibitions and art workshops. Due to construction works going on at their current location, some of their operations have moved to the National Theatre. Many courses, workshops and exhibitions are held there from time to time. They can be reached at 02 657 6171.

Sheikh Zayed Grand Mosque

www.visitabudhabi.ae/en; 800 555

A marvel of architecture, this is not only one of the largest and most awe-inspiring places of worship in the world, but the final resting place of the beloved father of our country. The Sheikh Zayed Grand Mosque opened in 2007 and features 82 domes. It has 1,096 columns with more than 20,000 handmade marble panels encrusted with semi-precious stones. The main prayer hall also features the world's largest hand-woven carpet (7,119 square meters) and the largest chandelier, made of Swarovski crystals. But numbers do not do this place justice. See it for yourself from 9am-8pm daily, except Friday mornings which are reserved for worshippers.

Guided tours are offered Saturdays-Thursdays at 10am, 11am and 5pm; Fridays at 2pm, 5pm and 8pm; as well as 2pm and 7.30pm tours on Saturdays. It is a wonderful opportunity to learn about our faith. As this is a place of worship, we ask you to dress modestly. Women will be provided with abayas, but should wear long sleeves and cover their knees. Men should not wear shorts.

Ferrari World

www.ferrariworldabudhabi.com; 02 496 8001; Yas Island

If you flew in to Abu Dhabi during the day, chances are you would have seen the enormous red roof of Ferrari World from the window. This world-class theme park opened in the capital in late 2010 and is a Ferrari-themed feast for the senses with heart-racing attractions such as the world's fastest roller coaster. There are many activities suitable for kids as this place is all about the family experience. Ferrari World offers an annual membership if you fancy being a regular or daily tickets for Dhs225 for adults and Dhs165 for children under 1.5m tall.

When you get tired of the rides, there are several Italian restaurants that offer a unique place to have a meal.

Yas Island is fast becoming *the* destination for entertainment, fun and sports. From Ferrari World to Yas Marina Circuit, to the Yas Links golf course and a Warner Brothers theme park in the pipeline, there's never a dull moment.

Emirates Heritage Village

02 681 4455; Corniche Breakwater

This is a great way to learn about our past and heritage – from our traditional hair houses (most people call them tents) to wind towers, our original method of air-conditioning, and, of course, our beloved camels. There are also small shops selling handicrafts including one in which bishts (robes) are made for the Sheikhs.

If you are a tourist, the village is a great place to visit and learn the history of the Emirates. If you live here, make sure you take your guests. Located next to the giant flag of the UAE, just south of Marina Mall, this is also one of the best places to take photos of the skyline. It is one of my favorite places to guide; look for my brown kandoura! It is open every day from 9am to 5pm and on Friday from 3.30pm until 9pm.

The Corniche

The place to go if you like to be outside is the Abu Dhabi Corniche. The path that runs along the Gulf is split into a bike path and a runners path. If you don't have your own bike, you can rent a two- or three-wheeler for Dhs20 an hour. There is also two kilometers of public beach that costs just Dhs10 (Dhs5 for children) for access. It is divided into a family area and a zone open to everyone. More than two dozen cafes, restaurants and shops line the beach.

Dine on a dhow

www.aldhafra.net; 02 673 2266

One of the oldest attractions in town, people can opt for dinner cruises either with a group, or rent a private dhow. Enjoy a lovely cruise whilst having a delicious Arabic dinner on board, not to mention the fresh seafood catch of the day.

Emirates Palace
www.emiratespalace.com; 02 690 9000; West Corniche

Most hotels in the world do not make it on to guide books' lists of attractions, but the Emirates Palace hotel is so much more than just somewhere to lay your head at night. Regardless of who you are or how long you are staying, this is the one place you must visit. Did you know this hotel was used as a stand-in for the Saudi presidential palace in the Hollywood movie The Kingdom? That's just how opulent it is. Just walking through the lobby you will see what all the hype is about. But this is not just a place for the wealthy to spend the night; anyone can wander through and enjoy a cup of coffee (sprinkled with gold leaf) or afternoon tea. Or, for a little more high brow entertainment, there are often art exhibitions and concerts – something for everyone.

Psst...

Abu Dhabi's past meets its future at the Saadiyat Island exhibition in Emirates Palace. Saadiyat, not even half a kilometer north-east of Abu Dhabi island, is scheduled to host some of the world's pre-eminent cultural institutions as well as a Gary Player golf course (which is now open), a marina and luxury residences. The exhibition takes visitors on a journey from Abu Dhabi's humble past to this future tourist destination. See what the "starchitects" – Lord Norman Foster (Sheikh Zayed National Museum), Frank Gehry (Guggenheim Abu Dhabi), Jean Nouvel (Louvre Abu Dhabi), Tadao Ando (Maritime Museum) and Zaha Hadid (Performing Arts Center) – have come up with and debate the merits of their blueprints and dioramas. The buildings will be part of a broader partnership with these institutions, which will include education, training and the sharing of exhibits.

Hyatt Capital Gate

www.abudhabi.capitalgate.hyatt.com; 02 596 1234; Khaleej Al Arabi Street

You don't have to go to Italy to see the Leaning Tower of Pisa. We have our own version, a leaning man-made tower operated by Hyatt hotel. This building is now one of the most recognizable landmarks in Abu Dhabi and has entered the *Guinness World Records* book as the farthest leaning man-made structure.

Ittihad Square

Airport Road, south of Hamdan Street

No tour bus goes through my city without stopping for a picture of the public artworks that make up an installation portraying symbols of Arab hospitality. They are a cannon, an Arabic coffee pot fountain, a rosewater vessel, a food cover and an incense burner. You might wonder how a giant cannon is a sign of hospitality. It's because we used to shoot it to signify the end of the fasting hours throughout the holy month of Ramadan when we didn't have microphones.

Sheikh Khalifa Park
Next to the Ministry of Labor, Al Salam Street
Of all the public parks in Abu Dhabi, this is the one you should choose if you're looking for a great family ambience. There is enough room in this new park for 5,000 people and enough activities to keep everyone happy. There are gardens and fountains and an amphitheater – and the best thing: it is all linked by a train.

Psst...

Don't miss the Abu Dhabi Maritime Museum located in Sheikh Khalifa Park. An electronic carriage takes you through a visual presentation of Abu Dhabi's history from pearling to the discovery of oil to the building of Abu Dhabi and the city's future. All in 10 minutes. It has one of the best aquariums in the city and tours are available in many languages.

Zayed Centre for Research and Studies

02 665 9555; Al Bateen

Previously known as the Man of Justice Center, this warm and authentic venue is one of my personal favorites. The center features the late Sheikh Zayed's personal photos, cars, gifts and awards. My favorite part is his personal collection of the most pure and expensive oud, the incense perfume he wore. The center is open daily from 8am-3pm, and Fridays from 4pm-8pm only.

Arabian Saluki Centre

www.arabiansaluki.ae; 02 575 5330; Al Shamkha, near Falcon Hospital

Our Arabian Saluki Center honors the Arab tradition by providing a professional, caring and friendly environment, where members and their Salukis can experience the latest and state-of-the-art services. It is indeed a place you have to visit if interested in the long-bodied and slim-statured Saluki hounds!

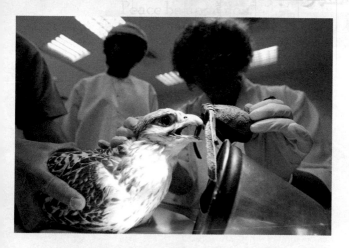

Abu Dhabi Falcon Hospital

www.falconhospital.com; 02 575 5155; Al Shamkha

You might have noticed a few falcons around town. They are everywhere, from our banknotes to the ADNOC logo. That's because they hold a special place in the hearts of Emiratis for the role they play in one of our favorite sports – falconry.

The Abu Dhabi Falcon Hospital is a great place to see these endangered birds. It is now the largest hospital of its kind in the country and has tended to over 35,000 birds, including raptors and pet birds. The hospital is especially concerned with reducing the transmission of bird-related diseases as well as training programs for veterinarians. Their tours take place on weekdays from 10am-12pm and from 2pm-4pm. Tickets cost Dhs170 per person and Dhs210 if you want lunch to be included. Call ahead to reserve your spot.

Attractions in Al Ain

Jebel Hafeet

Jebel Hafeet, or Mount Hafeet, is one of the main attractions to explore when you are in the city of Al Ain. It rises to 1,180 meters high on the outskirts of Al Ain at the border with Oman. This is a great place for trips with family and friends.

Mubazzarah Park (Green district)

03 783 9555; Mubazzarah

At the foot of Jebel Hafeet lies a heavenly place known for its greenery. Hands down, this is best place to enjoy our lovely winter. Take your friends and family out there for a lovely picnic, barbecue or a day of outdoor activities. Dip your feet into the hot springs, and enjoy the feeling of warmth rushing through your body.

Al Jahili Fort

03 764 1595; Jahili Area, General Park

Founded by Sheikh Zayed the First in 1898, the fort was recently restored as a cultural center and tourist attraction approved by UNESCO. When it was built, it was home to the ruling members of the Al Nahyan family, and then as a place for Abu Dhabi dwellers who escaped the heat of the city for the more tolerable weather in Al Ain. The fort houses a permanent exhibition for the explorer and traveler Wilfred Thesiger (aka Mubarak bin London), who crossed the Empty Quarter twice back in the 1940s.

Camel Market

Al Ain has the one-and-only permanent camel market in the UAE. The new location close to Al Bawadi Mall allows the animals to be kept in shade, while the facilities for traders are much more convenient. The market also has other livestock for sale, too.

Psst...

In the Arab world, camels are known to have more than 1,000 names. There are specific names for female and male camels, and common names given to both genders. For example, when it comes to the characteristics of a camel, there are names given also to those who have a different way of drinking water: Al Gasreed for a camel that does not drink much water; Al Ghab for a camel that drinks once every two days; Al Rab'e for a camel that drinks every three days; Melwah for a camel that is always thirsty; and it goes on and on.

Art galleries

The art scene in Abu Dhabi is beginning to flourish, with a little help from Abu Dhabi Art (www.abudhabiartfair.ae), a four-day event bringing in art from the region and the world.

Ghaf Gallery

www.ghafgallery.com; 02 665 5332; Al Khaleej Al Arabi Street
Named after a tree indigenous to this area, this gallery is not only in a great location, but is a great space, with 450 square meters of display area for international and local artists. What I like the most is that it exhibits work from young artists, including those studying at Zayed University and Abu Dhabi Women's College. The gallery is run by my artist friend, Jalal Luqman, and his partner, Mohammed Kanoo.

Psst...

Every year Luqman takes 10 non-established painters, photographers, sculptors, and digital artists on a journey through the UAE to educate and inspire them. Then he displays the results at the Ghaf Gallery. Look for details about future art trips on its website.

For a list of Abu Dhabi art galleries, visit www.ask-ali.com.

Tours

Let me share the route I would take you on as my guest if I only had a couple of hours. These are just suggestions, and tours can always be customized to include the sites and stops you are most interested in.

The first stop would be the Sheikh Zayed Grand Mosque (see page 129) to glean insights into our faith. Then we would drive to Mina Port to see the fruit and vegetable market, the date market and the fish market. This is a great place to take pictures of the many dhows – traditional Arabic sailing boats – that have played an important role in the development of our economy. Then we would cruise along the Corniche, with a stop to take pictures along the Breakwater, with its superb view of the city's skyline. We would stop, also on the Breakwater, at the Heritage Village (page 132), where you can see how my ancestors lived. Back on the island, we would circle Qasr Al Hosn (page 128), the old presidential palace, before stopping at the Emirates Palace (page 134) to marvel at its opulent architecture.

Birdwatching tours

Emirates Bird Records Committee; www.uaebirding.com
My country is one of the top four destinations in the Middle East for birdwatching. The Arabian babbler, Arctic skua, barbary falcon, black-crowned finch lark, Bonellis eagle, booted warbler, brown-necked raven, Caspian gull, little green bee-eater and eastern pied wheater are all species found in the UAE. Ornithologists may find these areas to be plentiful: Bateen Wood, Mushrif Palace Gardens, Eastern Lagoon, the Corniche, Al Ghar and Al Wathba. The Emirates Bird Records Committee runs customized tours on weekends, where experienced birders can email a list of species they would like to spot and the guide will plan the route accordingly.

Big Bus tours

www.bigbustours.com/eng/abudhabi; 800 244 287

You know a city is a rising tourist destination when it has its very own double-decker bus tour. The two-and-a-half-hour tour of the capital has 11 stops including the Sheikh Zayed Grand Mosque. If you're a morning person, service begins at 9am, but if you were out late enjoying Abu Dhabi's nightlife, you can pick up a bus any time until 5pm. Your ticket is valid for a full 24 hours, so if you want to cut your trip short, your ticket is valid the next day.

The Dhs200 ticket includes a bottle of water, access to the Sky Tower at Marina Mall (a nice vista of the city) and headphones so you can listen to commentary in English, Arabic, French, Italian, Russian, German, Spanish or Mandarin.

Seacruiser
www.seacruiser.ae; 050 800 9495
Yasser, a good friend of mine, recently launched Seacruiser. This is one of the few companies certified by the Abu Dhabi Tourism Authority to operate as local-licensed entertainment and a boating cruise company. He is passionate about his job and an expert of the waters. He can take you to many spots like the Breakwater, the Corniche, Sheikh Zayed Grand Mosque and nearby islands.

Mangrove tours
www.noukhada.ae; 050 721 8928
The mangroves in Abu Dhabi are a perfect place to catch a glimpse of the extent of biodiversity in the Emirates. Best explored in a kayak, the gentle waters make the trip an easy one even for the inexperienced. Fish jump from the water, birds swoop overhead, and crabs scuttle to and fro. After turning a corner to enter a channel lined with trees, the noise of the city disappears and you enter a whole new world. If you do not already own a kayak, or would prefer the assistance of a guide, call Don Revis from the Kayak Club Abu Dhabi. Patient and good humored, Don enjoys helping people explore this forgotten corner of the capital while championing the protection of the wildlife that lives here.

Learn Arabic calligraphy

www.adach.ae; 02 657 6355; National Theatre Building

A fun way to learn about our culture is to take a calligraphy course through the Abu Dhabi Culture and Heritage Authority. This art form has played an integral part in the history of our faith, as the holy Quran was first written in Arabic. ADACH also offers workshops in painting, photography, sculpture, ceramics, silk, fabric and glass painting, art jewelry design and fashion design. Training courses run from 8am until 8pm, Sunday to Thursday, and from 10am on Saturdays.

Skatepark
Corniche, next to Hilton Baynunah Hotel

Oh my, not only are they cycling in kandouras, but they are also wearing my favorite color, brown. The fact that we play some sports in kandouras doesn't bother us at all; if anything, we like to make it challenging. Let your kids sharpen their skating skills in this spacious skatepark on the Corniche. Whether they like to skateboard, rollerblade or bike, they can tackle ramps according to their level. It's a great place to get your adrenaline pumping. There is also a basketball court for ball enthusiats. The skatepark is right in front of the Hilton Baynunah, one of the oldest landmarks on the Corniche, recognizable by its dark blue glass and golf ball on top.

Fly a simulator plane

www.mutahida.com; 02 556 8555 / 055 411 0300;
Al Bateen Executive Airport

This activity reminds me of myself when I thought I wanted to be
a pilot back in the old days. At least now I can get to experience
what it feels like to be one! Mutahida Simulators offer you an
unforgettable experience in which you learn how to taxi, fly and
smoothly land a simulator. All for only Dhs350 per hour.

Go to an equestrian event

The Abu Dhabi Equestrian Club has 250 air-conditioned stalls and
hosts a number of prestigious racing events such as the National
Day Cup, the President's Cup and the Emirates Cup. From October
to April, Sunday is race day, with events from noon until 10pm. The
venue also hosts a number of showjumping events on its course,
modeled after the famous British Hickstead, including an annual
international show. Alternatively, you could watch a game of polo at the
Ghantoot Racing & Polo Club, about 45 minutes outside Abu Dhabi.

Cycling at Yas

www.ymc.ae; 800 927; Yas Island

Yes I know, we have limited cycling-friendly streets, but don't
worry, in addition to the impressive cycling paths on the Corniche,
the Yas Marina Circuit is dedicating its racetrack on Tuesday
evenings for bikers and runners. Entrance is free.

Psst...

If you want to take some riding lessons, then the
Dhabian Equestrian Club might be your choice. Check
out its Facebook fan page or call Tina on 050 662 0969.
Proceeds from the lessons go to its animal rescue center.

Experience the sea
www.empros.ae; 02 673 6600; Mina Zayed
You have no excuse not to cool off during the summer months by trying out our waters. From diving to fishing and even lazing about on a yacht, Empros offers all these activities and more for you and your friends.

Paintball
www.afoc.mil.ae; 02 441 5900 ; Armed Forces Officers Club
Paintball can be great fun and the big playground at the Officers Club will give you the space and safety to enjoy a round of colorful play. Games can include anywhere from six to 40 players. Prices start from Dhs150 per person, including safety gear and 100 paintballs. Reservations are necessary; a day ahead for weekdays and three days ahead for weekends.

Top up your tan in Al Gharbia

www.algharbia.ae; Mirfa Beach, Western Region

Al Mirfa public beach is the Western Region's only developed beach and best kept secret. Spend the day building sand castles or even stay the night to camp. It's quiet and peaceful, so you can enjoy sleeping out in the open.

Play sports under one roof

www.alforsan.com; 02 556 8555;
Khalifa City A, next to Abu Dhabi Golf Club

What better way to let out your energy than with sports and fun activities all in one place? Al Forsan is a newly opened club offering shooting, equestrian, paintball, motorsports, watersports and wellness under one roof.

Attend an exhibition

www.adnec.ae; 02 444 6900; Khaleej Al Arabi Street

ADNEC is Abu Dhabi's main hosting venue for over 100 regional and international exhibitions per year, in addition to shopping and summer festivals. Its facilities are modern and the venue can also accommodate other engagements. Many of the elite locals like to hold their weddings in ADNEC due to its spaciousness and flexibility to accommodate customized requirements for lavish events.

Rent a yacht

It doesn't hurt to pamper yourself every once in a while, so why not rent a yacht if you want? You can book it for the day to go on a cruise, or even hold your engagement party on board.
Call 050 699 9338 and ask for Captain Salem.

Watch a movie

You will always see nationals at the cinemas around town because we love movies. In fact, Abu Dhabi is aiming to be a world-renowned film production center as evidenced by the US$500-million deal the Government signed with Warner Bros. There are theaters at Abu Dhabi, Khalidiya, Marina, Al Mariah and Al Raha Beach malls. We even have two Bollywood theaters, The National (02 671 1700) and El Dorado (02 676 3555).

Psst...

Watching a movie here might be an experience for you, my expat friends. Some of us think of the movies as a place to congregate and socialize rather than the church-like behavior found in western theaters. It's a more relaxed culture. You might notice some people show up late and take calls on their mobiles. If this bothers you, please ask the offender politely to keep it down. Another tip: take a sweater, the conditioning in some theaters can make for Arctic temperatures.

Visit Manarat Saadiyat by TDIC
www.saadiyat.ae; Saadiyat Island

This venue is one of the nicest cultural exhibition venues in Abu Dhabi. Go there if you're looking to be taken on a journey through Abu Dhabi's past, present and future to showcase Saadiyat Island's future vision as the art and cultural hub.

Art workshops

www.adach.ae; 02 6576355; National Theatre, Manhal Street

If you're in the mood to take up some art courses or want to enroll your child in some, the Abu Dhabi Authority for Culture & Heritage is organizing several classes, including photography, Arabic calligraphy, art jewelry design, sculpting and much more.

Lose yourself with books

www.szgmc.ae ; 02 441 6444;
Sheikh Zayed Grand Mosque Center, 3rd floor

What a treasure! The Sheikh Zayed Grand Mosque Center library showcases books on Islamic architecture, Islamic art, rare Arabic calligraphy collections, and copies of the holy Quran printed in the West that are more than 400 years old. It is open Sunday to Wednesday from 8am to 8pm, Thursday from 8am to 4pm and Saturday from 9:30am to 4:30pm. It is closed on Fridays. Some books can be borrowed if you wish to take them home as well.

Watch camel racing

If you want a story to tell your friends back home, head to Al Wathba Racetrack (30km south east of Abu Dhabi). There, camels race long distances with robot jockeys controlled remotely by their owners, who drive alongside the camels in their SUVs. It is fascinating to see, because it's very different from horse or greyhound racing. Races are run all year, except for the summer when it is too hot for the camels (and maybe the robots too!).

Check out www.visitabudhabi.ae for updates on group trips to see the races or call the Camel Racing Department at 02 583 9200.

Psst...

Qais Sedki, my good friend, published the first Emirati manga book, "Gold Ring". His aim was to encourage reading and love Arabic through his sketches that portrayed our heritage and values. If you are intermediate in Arabic, try reading this book with your kids for a fun self-help lesson in Arabic. It will soon be released in English in major bookstores.

Things to do in Al Ain

Al Ain Zoo
03 782 8188; next to Jebel Hafeet

Al Ain Zoo is one of the most well-known zoos in the UAE. It has a vast collection of wild animals and an aquarium that was opened in 1967 by the late Sheikh Zayed. I have fond memories of being fascinated as a child by everything from the exotic gazelles to the extraordinary reptiles. The latest additions to the zoo are two white tigers, which are rare to see in their natural environment.

Psst...
The best way to make sure you've gotten around the whole zoo is by catching a free ride on the train. Be sure to check out the timings, as they change with the season.

Fly in a hot air balloon

www.ballooning.ae; 04 285 4949

Here is an excuse to wake up before dawn; go up in a hot air balloon to observe the beauty of my country. Surprise your spouse or friend with this unforgettable experience. The take-off point is in Al Ain, but don't worry, transportation is free of charge. If leaving from Abu Dhabi, all you have to do is drive to Carrefour on Airport Road.

Visit an oasis

03 763 0155; near Al Ain National Museum

The Al Ain oasis is made up of thousands of date palms. Although driving through is pleasant due to the narrow roads, walking along the date palms and listening to the birds is a lot more calming, especially since the trees offer plenty of shade.

Get active

www.palmsportsresort.com; 03 702 6405; near Tawam Hospital

Al Ain residents need not feel neglected when it comes to having an outlet for sports. The Palm Sports Resort offers a variety of activities to energize your life, including golf, rugby, equestrian and shooting.

Stroll through Zayed Walk

Next to Al-Jimi Bridge

This newly built walking area in the green city of Al Ain is beautifully done with trees planted along the walkways and benches for people to rest on. There are games for children to play and facilities for people with special needs.

Activities

If you were an avid athlete at home, there is no reason to give it up when you move to Abu Dhabi. There are facilities for most mainstream sports and lots more obscure ones, too. Lots of expats also decide to try a new hobby when they move because it is an opportunity for a fresh start.

Soccer

www.thedome.ae; 050 662 7701 / 02 449 8480;
Rawdhat, near Al Bateen Airport

Our sizzling summer can sometimes stop you from playing soccer in the outdoors because of the unbearable heat. The Dome is a state of the art indoor facility that allows all ball lovers to continue pursuing their passion. There are male and female changing facilities, so everyone can even have their fair share of playing the fields.

Yoga

India has arrived in the UAE. These two studios offer instruction in the physical and mental discipline, including women-only classes.

Yoga Tree
www.yogatree.ae; 02 667 6579;
Al Khaleej Al Arabi Street and 11th Street
Yoga Tree offers Hatha, Ashtanga, Vinyasa and gentle yoga as well as belly dancing and ballet lessons. Classes cost Dhs60 for one hour and Dhs65 for 90 minutes. A 10-class pass costs Dhs540 and private sessions are Dhs250 per hour. The studio does not operate in the summer.

Yogalosophy
02 495 2070; One to One Hotel, Al Salam Street
Has eight teachers and up to five daily classes, including one-hour "power lunch" classes, from 12:30 pm to 1:30 pm. One hour class costs Dhs30 for members of the Village Club gym and Dhs40 for non-members. For 10 sessions, it costs Dhs400 for members and Dhs450 for non-members.

The Yellow Boats
www.theyellowboats.com; 800 8044
If you love thrill boat rides, then you'll be happy to know that you and your family can slice through the waters with this fun activity. The Yellow Boats offer a range of reasonably priced packages in three different locations around Abu Dhabi. You have no excuse to stay in during the weekend now.

Go-karting

www.ymc.ae; 800 927 / 02 446 0384; Yas Island

Go-karting is a lot of fun when you do it in groups; there are special packages designed for how long you want to race. Shall I give you a tip? Try limiting your use of brakes when making sharp turns. That way your car won't drift and you will manage to shave off time and possibly win the race.

Kids Park

www.kidsparkuae.com; 02 563 3100; Al Bahia

This is a place that my little nieces love to go. Kids Park is a combination zoo and park with fun rides to keep all children entertained. What I like about this place is that some animals are safely placed in areas where they can move around and have children experience some interaction with them. Kids Park is located out of town in Al Bahia. Call for exact directions.

Psst...

At Kids Park, there is a dare game that your kids can play if they are brave enough. If they agree to let a snake rest on their shoulders (non-venomous, of course) then their friends get to clap and cheer for them.

Expressions Dance

www.expressions-dance.com; 02 448 2778; Muroor Road

Expressions Dance is a diverse dancing school, as they teach many dancing styles including ballet for kids. The instructors are certified professionals in their respective field, so be sure that your kids will be in good hands. The good thing about them is that they operate in 5 different branches in Abu Dhabi, so you can choose the one closest to you.

Ice skating

It might be 35°C outside, but that doesn't mean you can't get a taste of winter on one of the city's ice rinks. Skating is only Dhs25 at Zayed Sports City (02 444 8458). You can also give the children a break from shopping at Marina Mall, which offers skate rentals as well as coaching.

Swimming

You've heard the expression "Go jump in the lake"? Well, in Abu Dhabi, when locals want to swim, we go jump in the Gulf! Seriously, there are some beautiful swimming spots around the island, including the newly refurbished Corniche, but when it comes to public pools, I'm afraid we come up a bit dry. I'm hopeful that with all the new projects in the city, more pools suitable for lengthy swims will spring up, especially since we plan to host major sporting events in the future.

In addition to the pools listed below, you can also check hotel apartments in the area to see if they have less expensive options.

The Al-Jazira Sports Club
www.jc.ae; 02 445 4455; Muroor Road and Al Saada Street
This sports club has an Olympic-length swimming pool with temperature control and an audio system. You can pay as you swim or join for Dhs300 per month. Contact Hisham Abdul Fattah at 050 264 9707 for more information.

The Officers Club & Hotel
www.afoc.mil.ae; 02 441 5900; near Sheikh Zayed Grand Mosque
The gym here covers 465 square meters; that's bigger than my apartment! The indoor Olympic-sized pool has separate swim times for women.

Psst...

Life's a beach in Abu Dhabi; the city has a great assortment of sandy places to work on your tan. Many of the beach clubs are owned by hotels, but that doesn't mean you have to miss out. You can pay a daily fee and try one out. If you like it, yearly memberships are the most cost-effective.

Water sports

Abu Dhabi is a beautiful place for water sports, and there are several places that provide instruction and facilities for all manner of sports from sailing to jet skiing. One of my favorites is the Abu Dhabi International Marine Sports Club (02 681 5566) on the Breakwater. Beginner, intermediate and advanced sailing lessons are available. Similarly, any level of kayaker can rent a boat or take lessons. Now you can see Abu Dhabi in a whole different way: from the water.

Diving

The Arabian Gulf is rich with marine life and thank goodness for that, otherwise we would not have the delicious hammour. However, when it comes to professional diving, you need deeper water to enjoy the experience. The waters of the Indian Ocean, off the emirate of Fujairah three hours' drive away, are just perfect. Al Boom Diving (04 342 2993) offers a wide range of diving classes for beginners and professionals. Here are some other local diving clubs:

Abu Dhabi Sub Aqua Club
www.abudhabisubaqua.com; 02 673 1111; The Club, Al Mina
Only available to members of The Club (page 167).

Al Mahara Diving Centre
www.divemahara.com; 050 200 2708; Mussafah

Cricket

Perhaps even more popular than soccer is cricket, probably owing to the thousands of expat Indians, Pakistanis and Bangladeshis living here. There are more than 800 players with over 60 teams registered with the Abu Dhabi Cricket Council (02 558 8331), which organizes the popular Abu Dhabi Duty Free Tournament every year. The Abu Dhabi Cricket Club hosts over 500 professional and amateur matches all year round. Invest in your skills and become a member at the club to enjoy several benefits apart from doing what you love.

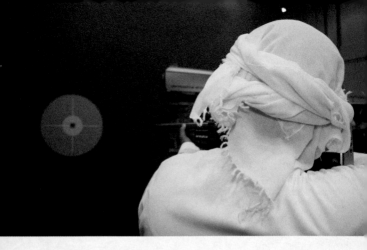

Shooting

Caracal Shooting Club; 02 441 6404; Al Khaleej Al Arabi Street
The city is home to its own pistol manufacturer, Caracal, which has its own shooting venue at the Armed Forces Officers Club. There is a state-of-the-art 25-meter range as well as a laser simulator for those not willing to handle a real gun, and a pro shop, where you can buy some of the products. Members can try their hand at Olympic-style pistol shooting, which is a traditional Arab sport.

Tennis

Night-time tennis is the norm here, because it can be so hot during the day. Almost all clubs are equipped with floodlights so you can play after dark when the temperatures drop. The Abu Dhabi Country Club (see page 166) has tennis courts, as does The Club (page 167), InterFitness at the InterContinental (page 65) and the Abu Dhabi International Marina and Yacht Club (02 644 0300). Prices vary, but courts cost about Dhs30 per hour on weekdays and Dhs100 during the weekend.

Bowling

I am not sure exactly why, but bowling is really popular here. It's surprising since it's not easy to throw a strike when you're wearing a kandoura. However, if you want to meet Emiratis, this is a great place to see us at our most relaxed. We even have a national team that does quite well in international

competitions. There are bowling alleys in almost every mall as well as at Zayed Sports City, where the Khalifa International Bowling Centre (02 403 4648) boasts 40 lanes and regulation table tennis tables.

Psst...

You're never too old to try a new sport or activity (although your chance of injury sure does go up). Duplays' (duplays.com; 055 224 0186) success in Abu Dhabi prompted its management to set up leagues for flag football, soccer, badminton, softball, tennis, cricket, beach volleyball and even dodgeball (which I only know from the movie). Games take place around the city, with venues in Khalifa City, the Sheraton Corniche and the Dome at Rawdhat, which is near the Sheikh Zayed Grand Mosque. Men and women can sign up, with leagues catering to all, from the person looking to start exercising to weekend warriors who want to go all out. (I'm thinking of Ben Stiller's character in Dodgeball!)

Golf

Despite our climate we still love green grass, and what better place to find the stuff than a golf course. Of particular note is the Abu Dhabi Golf Club (www.adgolfclub.com; 02 558 8990). With its famous falcon clubhouse and terrific golf course carved right out of the sand, it's not to be missed. Less prestigious but with its own unique charm is the Abu Dhabi Golf and Equestrian Club (www.adec-web.com; 02 445 9600; Al Saada Street). Set in the middle of the race track at the Equestrian Club, this challenging nine-hole grass layout can be played from two sets of tees. As a bonus, the course is floodlit so golfers can hack at it when the sun goes down. But if you really want the true desert golf experience you should head to Al Ghazal Golf Club (www.alghazalgolf.ae; 02 575 8040; near the airport). The front nine is modeled around an archeological site that used to be Abu Dhabi's old coastline, and instead of greens it has "browns", specially compacted and treated sand, to putt on.

Yas Links golf course (www.yaslinks.com; 02 810 7777) is the place to be if you want to lose yourself in a round of 18 holes. Work up your appetite and then dine at Hickory's. The delicious food blew me away, and if the weather is gorgeous, ask to be seated on the terrace.

At Saadiyat Beach Golf Club (www.sbgolfclub.ae; 02 557 8000), the 18-hole masterpiece of a golf course was designed by the legendary Gary Player. Abu Dhabi is growing fast as a world-class golfing hub, so get your clubs and start teeing off.

Health clubs

Abu Dhabi Country Club

www.adhfc.com; 02 657 7777; Al Saada Street

Your workout routine need never be boring with all the facilities available at this sprawling center. Besides two large gyms – one for women only – both with all manner of weights and cardio machines, the club features two swimming pools, tennis courts, basketball courts, squash courts and even bowling alleys. There are a wide variety of classes, from aerobics to yoga to spinning, and afterwards you can relax with a massage or in a Jacuzzi. The group fitness courses are amazingly engaging, fun and to be honest, a lot more entertaining than using gym equipment. But the craziest feature here has to be the indoor skydiving simulator. You'll see the tall tower at the gates of the club. I dare you to try it!

Skyline Health Club

02 632 7777; Hilton Baynunah, Corniche Road near Family Park

Take in one of the best views of the city and get in shape doing it. The Skyline is located on the 29th floor of Abu Dhabi's first skyscraper, erected in 1994. It has a small but complete weight room, a stretching area and cardio machines with a fantastic view of the Corniche. There is also a swimming pool that is perfect for laps.

Psst...

There are less fancy gyms around, too. If you want to train like Rocky in Rocky III, there are many body building and more basic health clubs in almost every district. Again, this is a question to ask your neighbors.

The Club
www.the-club.com; 02 673 1111; Al Mina
You know a place is popular if it's been around since before the UAE was a country. That's right, The Club (aka The British Club) has been bringing people together in Abu Dhabi since 1962! This space is located right on the port, offering a great view of the city from its beach. The Club offers all kinds of sporting activities – tennis, squash, badminton, diving, swimming, you name it – and also has its own library, hair salon and dry cleaners.

Groups and organizations

Many of my expat friends have found that joining a group has been a great way to help them adapt to life in Abu Dhabi. You might meet people who have been through the moving process and have tips (some of them might even be better than mine!) Here are just a few of the many groups and organizations I know about around town.

Abu Dhabi Mums
www.abudhabimums.ae
Raising children can be difficult at the best of times, never mind when you're in a foreign country. This informal community gives mothers of children under the age of six a place to share information and find support.

Abu Dhabi Women's Group

www.abudhabiwomensgroup.com; 050 132 8062

If you're up for meeting people and making new friends, this is the group to join. They regularly meet for coffee mornings, out-of-town trips and even indulge in group activities like golf and bowling. The beauty of this group is its multicultural members, which is perfect as you will learn a lot.

Damas Latinas Abu Dhabi

latina.abudhabi@gmail.com; 050 532 3994

Habla español? Spanish-speaking senoritas are invited to join this social club of over 100 members. They have a library of Spanish books, offer cooking classes and a play group for young children.

Abu Dhabi Speaks

www.facebook.com/#!/ADspeaks

Abu Dhabi Speaks is a group of mixed native speakers from different languages and nationalities who come together to learn a new language. The idea is to try and learn or improve your conversation skills in the language of your interest in an informal and friendly environment. At the end everyone is encouraged to try a few words for a fun challenge.

They meet every two weeks at Mockamore in Marina Mall from 6.30pm to 8.30pm. Speakers from all languages living in Abu Dhabi are welcome to join for conversation. They try to speak for 30 minutes in each language and it's free to join. So you have no excuses now.

Zen the Spa
02 697 9333; Beach Rotana Hotel
Zen should, as its name suggests, put you in a peaceful state of mind. Besides the usual wraps, facials and aromatherapy treatments, the spa offers a massage with two therapists instead of the usual one, I suppose to double your bliss. There are 10 treatment rooms and two relaxation rooms.

Chi
02 509 8900; Shangri-La Hotel
Another spa that takes its inspiration from the Far East, Chi is named after the Chinese word for the body's energy. As you might guess, the 10 treatment rooms, herbal steam room and hammam all have an Asian theme. Chi also offers special treatments tailored to the sensitive skin of us men.

Spa Essence
02 643 0201; Spa on Roof, Vision Tower 2, Najda Street
A large and well-equipped beauty and skin care center on the rooftop of one of the nicest towers in town with a big balcony and a beautiful view over the city. Massages, masks and wraps, body scrubs, facials, whitening, fat reduction and anti-wrinkle treatments are all available.

Eden
02 644 6666; Le Méridien

Eden puts an emphasis on mineral treatments, from baths to wraps. It also has a Turkish bath and all the pampering treatments you would expect. Try their Ayurvedic treatments; the Indian techniques will refresh and heal you.

Skyline Massage Treatment Centre
02 634 0616 / 02 632 7777; Hilton Baynunah

The Thais are known for their marvelous massage techniques and this center features a Thai practitioner. The Skyline is a very popular place with nationals who need to unwind. Run by Fusako Nakamura of the Japanese Sports Centre, this spa also offers aromatherapy and traditional relaxing massages.

Man/Age
02 681 8837; Marina Mall

Man/Age opened in 2008 and has slowly built a loyal clientele with its super-friendly service and excellent treatments. Men can pamper themselves with a haircut, manicure, pedicure or massage. And you are always offered a juice or tea to calm you further. Particularly recommended is the hot stone massage, which really takes the edge off a stressed body.

Abu Dhabi Classics
www.abudhabiclassics.com

In its effort to build Abu Dhabi's reputation as the Middle East's culture capital, the Abu Dhabi Authority for Culture and Heritage has consistently put together a line-up that rivals that of any major world city. Think I'm kidding? In the 2010/11 program, we had the world-renowned cellist Yo-Yo Ma and also performances from London's BBC Concert Orchestra conducted by Keith Lockhart. There are also programs for the young ones such as opera for the kids, where you can introduce your children to the wonders of classical music. Chances are if you haven't seen your favorite artist in your home country, you will see them here.
(April – May)

Abu Dhabi Art Fair
www.abudhabiartfair.ae

Ever since its launch two years ago, this event has drawn many people who are passionate about art. What's interesting about Abu Dhabi Art Fair is that it is not just an exhibition, but also a platform for so many workshops and seminars that attendees can benefit from. Furthermore, it places high importance on local and regional talent as there has been a lack of support in the past. Hopefully, with Abu Dhabi's 2030 vision, the capital will be one of the best art and culture hubs by then. **(Mid November)**

Al Dhafra Camel Festival
www.aldhafrafestival.com

The inaugural edition of this festival four years ago made international news, and for good reason. Souqs, poetry competitions, date competitions and, of course, camel auctions and camel beauty contests – all set against gorgeous desert scenery. What could be better?

If you want to see Emirati camel farmers in their environment, this is a great place to start. Camel herders bring their beasts from all over the Gulf, lending the event an amazing party atmosphere. Come, share a cup of Arabic coffee and find out what makes a camel the "ship of the desert". **(Mid December)**

Liwa Date Festival (Western Region)

www.liwadatesfestival.ae; 02 657 6094; Liwa, Western Region

The Liwa Date Festival is held annually in the Western Region of Abu Dhabi. It's an eight-day event that aims to preserve heritage and culture, where thousands of participants compete on the quality of dates they produce, while also educating farmers on palm tree preservation. The event is rich in cultural activities such as folkloric performances and traditional handicrafts, awareness lectures on palm trees and even group weddings! It's perfect for an educational outing with family and friends. **(Mid July)**

Abu Dhabi International Book Fair

www.adbookfair.com

Known as ADIBF, this annual five day event is for all the bookworms out there. It is held in ADNEC and is a place where you not only get to buy books, but also meet authors and poets, and attend interesting discussions and dialogues with people from the publishing industry. It's a good time to take your family as there is something for everyone. We launched the first edition of this guide at ADIBF in 2010. **(Mid March)**

Abu Dhabi Film Festival

www.adff.com

As I said before, Abu Dhabi is becoming a destination for film production. To cultivate this, as well as promote regional films, the Abu Dhabi Authority for Culture and Heritage hosts a lavish film festival each year. The 2010 festival attracted a host of Hollywood films and stars including Adrian Brody and Uma Thurman, as well as those from closer to home. Parties are as much a part of the festival as the films, and Abu Dhabi glams up its many flashy venues for the occasion. (**Mid October**)

Psst...

If you would like a once in a lifetime opportunity to work with the stars, visit ADFF's website (www.adff.com) and apply to join as an employee or a volunteer. You might just get lucky!

UIM F1 Powerboat Race

www.adimsc.ae

The Abu Dhabi International Marine Sports Club was founded in 1993 to help develop the city's water sports scene so it would be able to host world-class events such as this one. Top powerboaters convene in Abu Dhabi as part of their world tour. Watch these speed merchants reach more than 220kph with the beautiful Breakwater as a backdrop. (**December**)

Gourmet Abu Dhabi

www.gourmetabudhabi.ae

This festival for epicureans brings in master chefs from around the world for two weeks of good conversation and delicious food. Learn how to cook from Michelin-starred chefs who give master classes to Abu Dhabi's chefs and interested gourmands. Or book a chair at one of the gala dinners or lunch parties; your tummy won't be disappointed. I tasted the most unusual and delicious date dishes here. This event is organized by the Abu Dhabi Tourism Authority. **(February)**

Abu Dhabi Festival

www.abudhabifestival.ae; 02 651 0300 / 02 651 0300

This celebration of art and music usually attracts some impressive names. 2010 marked the seventh anniversary and happened to coincide with what would have been the composer Chopin's 200th birthday. I wonder what he would have thought about gangsta rap. The festival has seen the likes of the Bolshoi Ballet and Orchestra, the Puccini Festival Opera and Wynton Marsalis. The festival is managed by the Abu Dhabi Music and Art Foundation. **(March – April)**

Abu Dhabi Grand Prix

www.yasmarinacircuit.com; 02 659 9800 / 800 927

This multimillion-dollar sporting event attracts crowds from all over the world. The race occurs annually, and features the longest straightaway on the circuit. In addition to the track, Yas Island is also home to the futuristic Yas Hotel (page 64). There are several other hotels on the island, with more to come. Good luck getting any sleep on race day. **(November)**

Psst...

Yasalam, which means wow or how cool, is the name of a series of cultural events and concerts that accompanies the big race. The 2010 line-up included Kanye West, Linkin Park, Prince and many more.

Desert Challenge
www.uaedesertchallenge.com

The Desert Challenge is another event that proves just how much Emiratis love their cars. This is one of the longest-running competitions in the UAE, dating back 18 years. Top cross-country drivers from around the world take their ATVs, cars and motorcycles out to do battle with their toughest opponent: the desert. (April)

Abu Dhabi HSBC Golf Championship
www.abudhabigolfchampionship.com

Golf fans will revel in the stellar field the five-year-old event has attracted: Roy McIllroy, David Lynn, Gareth Maybinn, and Matteo Mannaserp, along with winner Paul Casey. But even if you're not a golf fan, the event has merit, as myriad sponsors set up booths for entertainment. (December – January)

Mubadala World Tennis Championship

www.mubadalawtc.com

The Mubadala World Tennis Championship takes place at Zayed Sports City and is considered a hit year-on-year. Emiratis and expats alike got to see six of the world's top 10 players, including Rafael Nadal and Roger Federer. In 2010, Nadal beat Federer to defend his championship title from the inaugural even in 2009. **(December – January)**

Summer in Abu Dhabi

www.summerinabudhabi.com

This entertaining family festival is organized by ADTA, taking place for six weeks at ADNEC. Breaking up the boredom of summer, this event provides kids with activities, live stage shows, competitions and much more to keep them busy. It's a great family event. **(June – August)**

Al Gharbia Water Sports Festival

www.algharbiafestivals.com;
02 404 4000

With a mandate to liven up the region with activities, here comes Al Gharbia's water sports festival. It occurs right before the onset of summer, so the weather is still good for working on your tan and enjoying a nine-day water-filled extravaganza of activities such as wakeboarding, surf skiing and kiteboarding, beach volleyball and beach soccer. **(April – May)**

Psst...

Just because you're not into water sports doesn't mean you should not go along with the family. There is a traditional souq set up for the women who are eager to burn some cash and stage shows to keep you entertained. It may just be a good chance to introduce yourself to the locals.

Tal Moreeb Festival

www.algharbiafestivals.com; 02 404 4000

If you really want to see the locals pumped up with adrenaline, this is one festival you MUST go to. It combines our love for the desert and cars, so you ought to see many of them camped out in the sand, some driving hard up the gigantic dunes and some gathered in groups around a bonfire watching the action. **(End of December)**

Local restaurants

These are restaurants you won't find in many city guides. They offer a great opportunity to see us Emiratis in our element and experience our dining culture. Plus, they serve up some pretty darn tasty dishes!

Al Arish
02 673 2266; Meena Souq; Al Mina fish market
A hidden gem that delivers an authentic experience, complete with Arabian hospitality. The restaurant uses fresh local ingredients and generous portions. Try Emirati dishes such as jesheed (baby shark), machboos, harees and biryani. Make sure you try the traditional starters and leave room for dessert. Eat at the tables that have aquariums on them or reserve the Royal Dining Room; the VIP room decorated in red and gold is excellent.

Nasser Restaurant
02 621 0482; Airport Road; next to Khalifa Hospital
If you're looking for good food without burning a hole in your pocket, Nasser Restaurant should be your choice. Their sweet corn soup and dish of fried chicken with rice is divine. My colleagues at the office like coconut beef strips with some chapatti (flat bread).

Psst...
Follow Lgeimat Junkies, a foodie blog run by the dynamic duo of Shaima and Latifa. They cook yummy food and write in a witty way. For inspiration on what to cook, just log on to blog.lgeimatjunkies.com and get in touch with them. They'll be happy to help.

Just Falafel

www.justfalafel.com; 02 626 2099; Hamdan Street, opposite Maha Arjan Rotana Hotel

What could be more satisfying than good, honest food that doesn't cost you an arm and a leg? For falafel junkies, this eatery offers all sorts of falafel in salads, sandwiches and various fusion sauces like avocado and cheese! One word: yum.

The seating area is tight, so it's best to have it delivered, or pass by for takeaway.

Dubai Special Kebab Grills

02 642 5566; Najda Street, opposite Ministry of Finance, next to Emirates Computers

Drop in to Abu Ali's joint and tell him I say hi. The many Emiratis who frequent Special Kebab all know and love the restaurateur (who has a son named Ali living in America, hence the name Abu Ali). As the name implies, the focus at this grill is on kebabs, but they also serve tikka and curry. Make sure you start with one of their soups – delish! The sultani is also worth a try, as is the rocca salad with chopped onion and cucumber. Best of all, dishes come with freshly baked Iranian bread. They also deliver.

The Goodie Bag

www.thegoodiebag.ae; 050 111 7160

I love to bake, but I have a hard time perfecting cookies because they either come out too crisp or too cake-like. This is where The Goodie Bag comes in. Run by an Emirati lady, she bakes the softest, most gooey cookies I have ever tasted, and they come packaged very nicely. Perfect for treating your colleagues.

Saudi Kitchen

02 642 5667; Gava Hotel, Defence Road

The focus here is on home cooking, Gulf-style, with great local dishes such as madfoon (a chicken or meat dish that is cooked in the ground) and mandi (a chicken and rice dish). You can order a takeaway pack or take a seat on the ground and eat as if you're in a local's home. A great place to experience the art of eating with your hand.

Psst...

My recent discovery from this restaurant is a dish called mathlootha, which comes from the word thalatha in Arabic meaning three. Basically this is a dish of three layers: thin flat bread topped with purred wheat and veggies and a layer of rice with grilled meat or chicken. It is simply divine with a side of rocca salad.

Lebanese Flower

02 642 1117; Defense Road

This restaurant is probably more popular here than it is in Lebanon. Every night, its outlets are packed with westerners, Emiratis and other Arabs. We love the high-quality grilled meats and fish, accompanied by freshly baked Arabic bread. Shawarma and falafel have now become part of Abu Dhabi cuisine. Service is efficient, a nod of your head will bring a bevy of waiters to your table, or even your car if you honk. There are also other locations in Khalidiya and the Tourist Club.

Habiba Al Nabulsi Sweets
02 666 9481; Al Khalidiya Street

When it comes to traditional Arabic sweets, I go to Habiba Al Nabulsi, which has by far the best rough or soft kunafa, a baked sweet with ricotta cheese. I recommend this place for dessert as it has a wide range of traditional Arabic sweet plates, from kunafa, shaybiyat, baqlava, maamul, which is served with dates, and qatayef to all kinds of cakes. As you can imagine, it is very busy during Ramadan. You can eat inside or outside, or take your sweets home.

Gulf Pastry
02 621 6611; Al Khalidiya Street

In Arabic we call this chain of restaurants Fatayer al Khaleej, and it's one of our favorites. Nothing fancy here, just tasty pastry topped with your choice of cheese, labneh, zaatar (a mix of herbs) with black olives or halloumi (a salty cheese). Gulf pastry also serves up small pizzas, shawarma and falafel. There are other locations at: Al Shahama Dubai Road; Tourist Club Area; Opposite Zayed University.

Al Khaizaran
02 448 6007; Muroor Road

For yummy home style Levantine and Gulf cuisine, order from Al Khaizaran. The specials of the day are filling, delicious and come with a complimentary green salad, lentil soup and bread. Not to mention its portions are good for two people. If you are super hungry, then don't share!

Traditional Emirati food

Emirati food is all about simplicity and richness in flavor. The key to our cuisine is a mixture of cardamom, ginger, cinnamon, black pepper, rose water, saffron and loomy (dried lemon). Thanks to my mom, Umm Ali (mother of Ali), for helping me put these recipes together.

Machboos

This is my ideal lunch, especially when its combined with yogurt and salad. It is made of rice, onions, chicken or beef and seasoned with loomy and other spices. The ingredients are boiled until tender  before adding rice and cooking together for another 30 minutes.

Harees

When there's a celebration of any sort, Ramadan, Eid or a wedding, it's always harees. Small pieces of meat, cracked wheat and water are boiled then blended into a thick paste similar to porridge. Pure joy.

Psst...

All meat in the UAE must be halal, or butchered in accordance with Islamic law. Animals should be slaughtered mercifully and be served without the blood. If you cook for a local. it's best to prepare the meat well done.

Also...

An excellent way to make friends is to offer us food. And when I say food, I mean home-cooked food. We appreciate it a lot! In our culture it is a symbol of goodwill and friendship. Just make sure not to include pork or alcohol (even in chocolates).

Thareed

This chicken or lamb stew prepared with carrots, potatoes, and marrow is served over pieces of very thin bread called regag. The smell always reminds me of Ramadan, as it's the dish I eat the most during the holy month.

Lugemat

Take one of these dough balls covered in date syrup and combine it with a cup of gahwa and you get a little slice of heaven. They are especially popular around Ramadan or at weddings and other celebrations.

Khanfarush

Sweet buns eaten as light snacks with tea. It's especially good when dunked in some chai.

Farni

A sweet pudding made from ground rice and milk. It's one of the desserts that we like serving to guests when they come over.

Balaleet

This is our version of an omelet, but much brighter because it contains saffron. This magical-looking breakfast is made of vermicelli pasta, eggs, onions, cinnamon, sugar and oil.

Asseada

This orange-colored dessert can be found in almost any majlis. It combines saffron with the unique flavor of pumpkin.

Batheeth

This dish of freshly ripened dates with sauce reminds me of dessert at my grandparents' house.

Gahwa Arabiya

You'll see the little cups for this coffee in most Arab homes. Coffee with cardamom and other spices is served in small portions from a special coffee pot. The coffee is a little bitter so we eat dates to sweeten the taste for contrast. We do not add milk. Emirati coffee comes in three types: yellow, red and black.

To make Gahwa Arabiya:

1. Boil water in a pot.
2. Add 4 tbsp of blonde coffee, roasted and crushed. Bring to a boil, then lower heat to let simmer and leave for five minutes.

To make it yellow: Add a few saffron threads before pouring into the coffee flask.

To make it red: Same method, but use brown coffee instead of blonde and a touch of saffron.

To make it black: Use dark coffee. No saffron.

Chai Karak (or chai haleeb)

A popular beverage translated as "tea with milk", usually taken three times a day for those addicted to its soothing and sweet flavor. It was introduced to us by our friends from India and it is now embraced as a local beverage.

Zanjabeel

We swear by this ginger tea with milk as a cure-all because it kills bacteria and germs. When we order the famous zanjabeel with lemon at a coffee shop, the waiter might say "Salamaat", meaning get well. "Allah yesal mak" is the correct reply and that means may God protect you, because ordering Zanjabeel sometimes indicates that you may have a sore throat.

Gahwa Turkiyah

Quite famous among us Arabs is the classic Turkish coffee. It is made by boiling ground, roasted coffee beans several times. The trees that produce this coffee bean can grow to more than three meters in height, in contrast to the South American plant, which only grows to a meter and a half.

For a list of Emirati recipes, visit www.ask-ali.com

Psst...

All types of coffee are called gahwa, but in restaurants or coffee shops it usually means American or Turkish. If the waiter asks how you would like your coffee, he is asking about Turkish. There are four answers: 1. Saada (no sugar), 2. Al reehah (a tiny bit of sugar), 3. Wassat (medium amount of sugar), 4. Hellwah (very sweet).

International restaurants

There are so many restaurants popping up around the city, it's impossible for me to list them all here. That doesn't mean you shouldn't try those I haven't mentioned and give me your feedback for future editions. I am just recommending places that I go to with my local and expat friends. Reservations are recommended, especially on Thursday nights and Fridays.

Havana Cafe
02 681 0044; Breakwater, opposite Marina Mall
This place is great in winter when the weather is cool enough for *al fresco* dining. The service is courteous and there is a shisha waiter to bring you a water pipe. A unique place to take in the city's skyline, especially at night when it's all lit up.

Le Cafe
02 690 8050; Emirates Palace
After touring the hotel, wind down with a cup of coffee served with gold leaf shavings in true Emirates Palace style. Also try the paprika-flavored french fries and the steak sandwich. Besides the delicious food, this is a great spot to see the celebrities who come to town. I once ran into Jamie Foxx and Richard Branson here.

Robusta Cafe
050 932 1230; Al Bateen / 02 553 2553 Mazyed Mall
To me, coffee is truly one of the pleasures in life, and this cafe, hands down, does it like no other barista does. It is owned by an Emirati who is beyond passionate about coffee making. Robusta recently took off after years of research and securing the right coffee farms abroad. The baristas are very educated about their product and will

be happy to suggest pairings of your drink with a certain dessert. Their branch in Al Bateen is Abu Dhabi's best kept secret. I took my colleagues there and they've been going back ever since. It is a very secluded spot from the drowning noise of the city, and you even get a view of the sea and the yachts at dock. Like I said, simple pleasures.

Galler
02 681 8566; Marina Mall
This was my makeshift office for two years. I wrote my book and came up with the idea for this very miniguide while sitting in this orange cafe in Marina Mall. I especially like the rocca salad with coconut curry chicken. It is also famous for hot chocolate, a nice break from coffee. Oh yeah, and don't forget to try the crêpes.

Silk Route Café
02 657 4888 / 02 657 4858; Holiday Inn, Muroor Road
You should know that I am a die-hard fan for everything Korean, and so is one of my colleagues. Every Thursday, Silk Route Café puts on a lavish Korean Night buffet. It's pretty good Korean food and attracts many Koreans; perfect for me to brush up on the language. Try my favourite dishes, bulgogi and galbi, which are a Korean variation on stir fried beef and ribs.

Marco Pierre White Steakhouse & Grill
02 654 3238 / 02 654 3333; Fairmont Bab Al Bahr
Yes, Marco Pierre White is in Abu Dhabi. His steakhouse is one of the best in town, and for such a legendary chef like him, make sure you pack your wallet when you go to his restaurant. I like to go there when I'm craving a good roast with Yorkshire pudding. There's a drink that really puts on a great show, it's a strawberry-mint juice topped with cotton candy that gets absorbed into the drink when lit on fire! Cool stuff. It's delicious, too.

Prego's

02 697 9125 / 02 697 9000; Beach Rotana Hotel

Prego's boasts a large, airy interior and a superb terrace over-looking the beach. The Italian food is wonderful and the menu includes charcuterie. Not only is it family friendly, but it's a great choice for an intimate dinner because there is loads of space between tables.

BiCE

02 692 4160 / 02 681 1900; Hilton Abu Dhabi

For modern Italian cooking with a touch of romance, BiCE is your place. The pasta is handmade and delicious, and served by friendly, knowledgeable staff. Pick a window seat for a view of the Corniche.

Vasco's

02 692 4328 / 02 681 1900; Hiltonia

A contemporary fine dining venue offering a fusion of European, Arabic and Asian cuisines, overlooking the water. The food is presented imaginatively and the service meets high standards.

Benihana

02 697 9122 / 02 697 9000; Beach Rotana Hotel

The contemporary Japanese cuisine will be what attracts you, but the real stars of this place are the crowd-pleasing teppanyaki chefs who prepare your meal on a grill right in front of you. Prices may seem high, but for a feast of melt-in-your-mouth treats and the showmanship, it is good value.

The Meat Co

02 558 1713; www.themeatco.com; *Souk Qaryat Al Beri*

If you are a fan of steaks and African grills, you will be a fan of The Meat Co, the South African steakhouse chain housed at the Souk Qaryat Al Beri next to the Shangri-La. While I go there for the juicy steaks, the seafood selection and appetizer dishes are definitely worth a try. And if you didn't know, staff at The Meat Co also love to sing. It's a favorite spot of mine to take visiting friends, especially for birthdays, as waiters and waitresses burst into African-style drumming and song on your special big day.

Psst...

The Meat Co in Europe is called The Meat & Wine Co. This goes to show that even corporations need to adapt and embrace cultural differences in other parts of the world in order to penetrate their market. Even though they still serve alcohol, they had to omit the word wine in their name to appeal to Islamic population, and it works like a charm.

Rodeo Grill

02 697 9126 / 697 9000; *Beach Rotana Hotel*

One of the best steak places in the UAE as far as I'm concerned. The venue is sublime and the service faultless. For all of Abu Dhabi's strengths as a dining destination, Rodeo Grill is one of the classic places to try.

Indian Palace

02 644 8777; *Defense Road*

If you are a fan of authentic Indian food then this place is a must. The food is extremely tasty and the portions are generous, offering good value for your dirham. I am never disappointed when I visit.

Finz

02 697 6350 / 02 697 9000; Beach Rotana Hotel

Abu Dhabi's only restaurant built entirely from wood overlooks the sea and offers fish just about any way you like it. Try the cataplana, which is a Portuguese specialty in which food is cooked and served in a large copper pan. Don't be put off by the black dinner roll served as part of the bread basket; it's made with squid ink.

Visit www.ask-ali.com for more ideas on great places to eat.

Psst...

Dinner does not always have to be in a restaurant. Get yourself onto a dhow so you can eat with the sea underneath you and the moon above. Could there be anything nicer? Cruises aboard the traditional wooden vessels will give you a different view of the city, both the modern and traditional aspects, as you cruise by the Corniche. Try the Shuja Yacht Cruise organized by Le Royal Méridien Hotel. Contact them for reservations at 02 674 2020.

Nightlife

Yes, we are an Islamic country, but we are aware that not everyone who lives here shares our non-alcoholic lifestyle. There are many different western-style jazz and piano bars, cocktail lounges and classic, time-honored British and Irish pubs, some of which have live music. Alcohol is haram (forbidden) for Muslims, so the places listed here are recommended by my best expat friends. But don't worry, I hang out with sophisticated expats.

Captain's Arms
02 644 6666 / 02 697 4482;
Le Méridien

A traditional English pub that never seems to have enough space. The place is always packed with revelers spilling beyond the outdoor patio. As well as serving up some classic pub grub, including fish and chips, they have a wide range of beers.

Hemingway's
02 681 1900; Hilton Abu Dhabi

One of Abu Dhabi's oldest hangouts, Hemingway's serves up South American food that the author of *The Old Man and the Sea* would appreciate. Try the nachos, they're amazing.

Psst...

A note about live music: Abu Dhabi has attracted international stars such as Beyoncé, Shakira, Sean Paul, Kanye West, Coldplay, Aerosmith, Guns N' Roses, George Michael and many more. Some artists also perform in Abu Dhabi for a smaller crowd, usually in the night clubs instead of bigger venues. Of those bars that do have live music, the talent varies in quality from some terrific Filipino cover bands to some not-so-terrific pub singers.

Cristal Cigar and Champagne Bar
02 626 2700; Millennium Hotel

As you might expect from a place with a name like this, this is an upscale venue with nice leather chairs and a fireplace. The pianist does excellent renditions of Frank Sinatra songs.

Trader Vic's
02 697 9114 / 02 697 9000; Beach Rotana Hotel

Abu Dhabi is certainly hot enough for this Polynesian style restaurant/bar. Lots of flowered shirts and sweet rum drinks make Trader Vic's one of the busiest bars in the city most nights.

Left Bank
02 558 1680; Qaryat Al Beri
The ambience at Left Bank is very modern with red leather banquettes and a crystal VIP pit. The cocktail list is lengthy, and the bartenders have all been trained by a world-renowned mixologist. There is an outside area with great views of the Sheikh Zayed Grand Mosque.

NRG Sports Bar
02 644 6666 / 02 697 4382; Le Méridien
Soccer unites the crowd at the city's best sports bar. Lots of television screens means lots of different matches play at once and they make a great steak sandwich to enjoy with your pint.

Jazz Bar
02 681 1900; Hilton Abu Dhabi
Scoobidy-wow-wow, cats and kittens! A six-piece jazz combo accompanies some great food and modern décor – a perfect place for a classy night out.

The Yacht Club
02 666 6888 / 02 693 5373; InterContinental
A hip place for the young and trendy. With a nautical-inspired decor, the whole place morphs into a nightclub under the watchful eyes and ears of the "mood guru". Don't forget to look up and check out the enormous fan: I guess they use it to keep things cool. If you want to get away from the club, just go outside, where comfy white couches overlook the harbor.

Etoile

02 690 7999 / 02 690 8960; Emirates Palace

Another fancy restaurant-turned-nightclub at the swankiest of Abu Dhabi's hotels. Chef Dean Bouvet creates the Michelin-rated cuisine, while the club has become a hit thanks to its groovy atmosphere and impressive lineup of top DJs. This is the place where Paris Hilton partied when she came to the city, so it must have something going for it.

Pearls & Caviar

02 509 8888 / 02 509 8885; Shangri-La Hotel

This round-shaped restaurant/lounge sits just out over the water. When the weather cools down, it becomes a popular hangout.

Hakkasan

02 690 7999 / 02 690 7739; Emirates Palace

This Michelin-starred Chinese fine dining restaurant is one of the best in the region. A perfect place for any occasion whether you want to dine in the restaurant or hang out in the lounge over some mouthwatering bites. I suggest you book in advance as it's always busy!

Psst...

Many of Abu Dhabi's finer night clubs have dress codes, which prohibit the wearing of T-shirts, shorts or baseball hats. Almost every bar also bans sandals, which I think is a not-so-subtle hint to locals to stay away.

Cafe culture

Some of us like to hang out at a maqha, watching football, talking and smoking shisha. So unless you are sensitive to smoke, pull up a chair at one of these cafes for an experience unique to the UAE.

There are two types of cafes: the maqha, which serves shisha, and the coffee shop, which does not. Both types serve beverages, but the coffee shop will usually have waiters who bring your drink in fancier cups. We usually decide where to hang out by where our friends are.

Strictly speaking, smoking shisha contradicts Islam, which frowns upon devotees harming themselves in any way. But the shisha cafe is to the Middle East what the pub is to England.

Contrary to popular belief, however, the water pipe did not originate in Arabia, but in ancient India. In fact, it is only in the Arab world where the water pipe is known as shisha or arjeela. Most other regions use the term hookah, which is closer to the original Indian name for the pipe.

Games

When we gather with our friends, we play various games like chess, cards and dominos. One of the games that our ancestors brought back with them from India is called kairam (carrom).

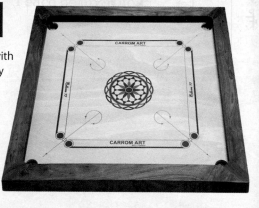

It is a very interesting game, but one that I'm not very skilled at. But when Emiratis get together in a majlis, it is not easy to resist challenging your buddies to a game of Kairam. It is a tabletop game (pictured above) that is perfect for playing with family or friends. I highly recommend buying one and perhaps after getting the hang of it, you can challenge a local to put your skills to the test.

Psst...

Besides chess, card games and PlayStations, we are die-hard fans of snooker and billiards. We are one of the sport champions on the professional circuit. Need I say, we have many ways for scoring when playing billiards too, so just make sure you state which method you are using. Don't cheat.

Shopping

We love our malls. They are an air-conditioned respite from the heat and a good place to congregate for coffee, a movie or just some people-watching.

Abu Dhabi Mall

www.abudhabi-mall.com; 02 645 4858; Tourist Club area
This was the first mall in Abu Dhabi. The three-story shopping center is located in the Tourist Club area, adjacent to the Beach Rotana Hotel. It houses everything from The Body Shop and Benetton to Mango and Mothercare. It also has some great dining spots and I enjoy all of the coffee shops there.

Marina Mall

www.marinamall.ae; 02 681 2310; Breakwater

Marina Mall is more than a shopping destination, it is a wonderful location for the entire family to visit and enjoy. It boasts a musical fountain and an ice rink, as well as a lightning strike that makes rain fall in some parts of the mall. It is located along the Breakwater near the magnificent Emirates Palace.

Khalidiyah Mall

www.khalidiyahmall.com; 02 635 4000; 26th Street

The mall rises in the midst of a bustling street, located in the residential area of Khalidiya. Architecturally inspired by Arabic styles, it is spread over an area of 86,000 square meters with space for 160 retail outlets.

Al Wahda Mall

www.alwahda-mall.com; 02 443 7070; Defense Road
The mall is close to my office and hence so helpful to me! Located off Airport Road beside the famous Al Wahda Sports Cultural Club, the mall houses more than 150 brands. Some of the major ones are Mamas and Papas, Gap, Banana Republic, Adidas, The Body Shop, Starbucks, Dome Cafe and a whole lot more. Also, you will find the biggest Lulu Hypermarket in the city here.

Fetouh Al Khair

www.marksandspencerme.com; 02 621 3646;
Airport Road and Hamdan Street
This shopping mall is anchored by Marks & Spencer, a classic British retailer. Most people call it the Marks & Spencer building, and it is known for its flower booth and lingerie shops. Duck out the back and you'll find yourself in the souqs along Hamdan Street.

Hamdan Center

Hamdan Street is one of Abu Dhabi's most bustling thoroughfares. You'll find expats hawking phone cards and roasting peanuts in front of the many, many shops. The street is particularly good if you're looking for DVDs, gold or low-priced clothing.

Khalifa Center

Opposite Abu Dhabi Mall, Tourist Club area

Cross the street from Abu Dhabi Mall to this unique center. Vendors sell everything from incense burners and oils to silverware and antique daggers. There is also a carpet souq and a place to get Arabian-flavored ice cream, such as saffron. It is the perfect place to find souvenirs to take home.

Al Mariah Mall

02 677 1741; Al Najda Street and Hamdan Street, near Le Royal Méridien

The curious mix of shops and restaurants in this mall draws a lot of nationals. On the bottom floor is the American family restaurant Chili's and a pet store. The first floor is home to many local shops you won't find anywhere else, including a music shop with cassettes of Arabic and Indian singers. That's right, cassettes. You'll also find a McDonald's and a Popeye's chicken. The second floor features a nine-screen multiplex that often screens movies that don't play at other cinemas. But the best part of this mall is the third floor: there are arcade games, laser tag and couches where you can play your favorite video game. On top of that is Bowling City, which obviously has a bowling alley, but also karaoke rooms, a pool hall and a snack bar.

Mushrif Mall

www.mushrifmall.com; 02 642 7100 / 02 690 4422; Mushrif

This mall will have one of my favorite things: an indoor market for veggies, fish and meat. Gone will be the days when I have to do it in the scorching heat of our summer. Better yet, my favourite seafood restaurant Jimmy's Killer Prawns is going to open there!

Mazyad Mall

www.mazyadmall.com; 02 553 2200; Mohammad Bin Zayed City

A shopping center with just the right number of convenience stores and a large supermarket is located in Mohammed Bin Zayed City to save the day. So if you live outside the city center, your weekly grocery will need not be a chore.

Dalma Mall

www.dalmamall.ae; 02 550 6111; Musaffah, next to ICAD

This shopping center is anchored by Carrefour and is the perfect place to do your monthly or weekly groceries if you live within the areas that are out of Abu Dhabi city, like Musaffah, Khalifa, Mohammed Bin Zayed, Baniyas, Shahama, Shamkha, etc. It has various brands and good restaurants to take your family to if you don't want to go all the way into the city.

Psst...

You will sometimes see a man holding his wife's hand in the corridors of the mall. That's because if he lets go, she might go to every store and shop! It may look romantic, but it's actually economic. Just kidding!

Shopping in Al Ain

Al Ain Mall

www.alainmall.com; 03 766 0333; next to Al Ain bridge

Yes, there's lots of good shopping – almost 200 stores and kiosks – but for me Al Ain Mall is all about the people-watching. Start with the ice rink, where everyone from beginners to experienced spinners and jumpers share the ice. Then check out the huge arcade, with everyone engrossed in their games. After grabbing a snack or a coffee, you can catch a film at one of the eight screens or bowl on one of 12 lanes.

Al Jimi Mall

www.aljimimall.com; 03 762 3859

Located on Government Road in the green city, Al Jimi underwent an extreme makeover a few years ago and expansion continues today. There are more than 100 stores, including the French hypermarket chain Carrefour, where you can buy almost anything. The food court is a highlight with 15 cuisines to choose from, but the real coup de grâce of Al Jimi is its outside area, with space for over 1,000 cars to park. In the UAE, that's a big deal!

Al Bawadi Mall and Souq

www.bawadimall.com; 03 784 0000

This is another modern souq (in the style of Qaryat Al Beri in Abu Dhabi) which hints at our Arab heritage while offering modern comforts and convenience. The Bawadi Souq features 55 traditional vendors, together under a unique curved structure on Mezyad Road that is right beside the mall of the same name, which is the biggest in Al Ain. The complex will eventually include a Fun Ski Village as well as a roller coaster. Woohoo!

Traditional souqs

Souq is the Arabic word for public market and a visit to at least one is a definite must-do for visitors. I promise you it offers a chance to soak up the atmosphere as well as find a few bargains. My grandfather told me that souqs were once like a maze of shady alleyways. Today they resemble a collection of small shops, but they still have the same buzz as their ancestors. Here are a few great ones in Abu Dhabi.

Qaryat Al Beri
Shangri-La Hotel; Between two bridges
This modern version of the souq mixes some hip new restaurants with boutique shopping. Attached to the luxurious Shangri-La Hotel, the souq is accessible by gondola, on the hotel's Venetian-style canals. The hotel overlooks the water and the Sheikh Zayed Grand Mosque, so it's a nice setting for a meal or coffee. There are various shops that sell local antiques and handicrafts.

Central Market

www.centralmarket.ae; 02 810 7810; Behind Fotouh Alkhair center

Historically, this used to be the main souq area where people came to shop and bargain for textiles, clothes, toys, spices, gold, you name it! I used to get dragged by my mother sometimes, and I'd never leave happy if she didn't buy me a toy and a shawarma. Hmm, I just realized how fussy I was! Unfortunately, there was an accidental fire and it wiped out most of the souq with it. It was then redeveloped into a modern interpretation of a souq that is indoors.

Psst...

Head down to my favorite café and chill out spot at the Central Market, Shakespeare & Co. As the name suggests, the décor of the café is somewhat Shakespearean, but it's still cosy. I go for the rocca salad and grilled baby chicken. OK, now I'm craving some. (Puts pen down and rushes off.)

Madinat Zayed Shopping and Gold Center

Muroor Road, next to Emirates Post Office

This vast retail complex offers shoppers pleasant air-conditioned surroundings, but don't think this is another mall. You won't find western outlets here, but unique shops selling clothes, perfumes, cosmetics, shoes, watches and electronics. Next door is a souq devoted entirely to gold. My country is a great place to get this precious metal at a good price. I have heard from my female expat friends who prefer to cover up for work that this is also a good place to buy affordable abayas and sheilas.

Psst...

Everyone wants a bargain; here's how to get one. First of all, don't use the word haggle; it sounds too stand-offish, the opposite of the way you should behave to get a discount. Try to be friendly; greet the shopkeeper with As salamu alaykum, which works no matter what language he might speak. Show a genuine interest in the goods he is selling, without coming across as a tourist. A good tactic is to ask what price an item would be if you purchased several. The next tip is to ask for the last price or discount by saying "kam akher". Don't expect the shopkeeper to do it. Finally, be prepared to walk away if you don't get your price. The shopkeeper will either stop you and negotiate or he will let you go. Of course, the best way to get a bargain is to build a relationship with the shopkeeper over time. You'll be surprised how many goodies you get when you are a regular.

Iranian Souq

Al Mina near the Fish Market

This stop is always an essential part of my city tours. The souq is an open-air traditional market where goods imported by dhow from Iran are displayed under awnings by friendly and enthusiastic traders. If you love home décor and want visitors to be impressed by your beautiful Persian carpet, then make this your destination. Exotic bedspreads and carpets in unique fabrics and designs are some of the best buys. You can also get pottery that you paint yourself. There is even a green nursery and amazing fish, and fruit and vegetable markets nearby. Bargaining is *de rigueur* and an essential part of the fun. Expect prices to drop by as much as 40 per cent from the original amount quoted.

Psst...

Since you are in the Middle East, you will want an Afghan or Persian carpet. I suggest you visit the carpet souq in the Mina area near the pet stores. Afghan and Pakistani salesmen will welcome you heartily and unfold as many carpets as it takes for you to say wow. Make sure you don't agree to the first price they name. Half the fun of visiting these stores is the bargaining. And don't worry about fitting your purchase into your suitcase. You will be amazed at how small they can fold your carpet.

Souvenirs

Gifts that say something about our culture and history are available at Emirates Heritage Village, the Khalifa Center, or gift shops in the malls.

Since Abu Dhabi means "father of the gazelle", you could pick up a statue or drawing of this graceful animal. A traditional bag made from palm tree leaves is nice, as is a box of khalas dates (in season from July to September). Pairing an Arabic coffee or tea pot with a set of cups with Emirati drawings makes a good souvenir.

For female friends or family members, you could buy a burqa or a beautiful sheila and abaya. A coffee table book on our city is always a good choice: *Abu Dhabi Life and Times – Through the Lens of Noor Ali Rashid* is a great one.

Psst...

When we visit people for an occasion, the most popular gifts we give are sweets, cakes and desserts from places like Fuala (02 642 0506) and Patchi (02 681 7554). These two shops are loved by the Emiratis.

Another original idea is to get someone's name written in Arabic and frame it, which I like to do for my expat friends. (Check out www.ask-ali.com to convert your name to Arabic.)

Finally, you can buy some oud perfume. This incense is well known in Gulf Arab countries, and we sell plenty, which we burn on coals when we get dressed. It gives off a lovely scent, which is called bukhoor.

Arjmst
www.arjmst.com

Azza Al Qubaisy is one of the pioneering Emirati jewelry and souvenir designers and silversmith. Her line, Arjmst, is an exquisite representation of antiques and pieces that embody symbols of the UAE. She also established "Made in the UAE" an exchange program to promote local handicrafts.

Women's Handicraft Centre
02 562 1918; Women's Association Complex; Karama Street

You will see for yourself how local handicrafts are made such as woven baskets, incense and perfumed Arabic oils. Of course, you can also buy a few souvenirs for your loved ones at home.

Petals
www.petalsfe.ae; 02 443 9880; Muroor Street; near NBAD

Flowers are a lovely way to celebrate a good occasion or even as a decor for your event. Owned by an Emirati, Petals is a flower shop that's quickly gaining popularity with the local ladies here. Check out this beautiful shop when flowers pop into your mind.

Psst...

Sougha is an initiative by Khalifa Fund that joined forces with elderly local women living in rural areas to promote their hand-crafted items using palm tree leaves known as "khoos" in Arabic. The items made are not limited to eco-friendly baskets and bags, but also mobile covers, tissue box covers, folders, laptop cases, key rings, etc. Their shop is set to open in the Central Market by spring 2011. So pop in and support their craftsmanship. For any queries, e-mail sougha@khalifafund.gov.ae or visit kfgateway.com.

Out-of-town excursions

Sir Bani Yas Island
www.desertislands.anantara.com; 02 801 5400

The late Sheikh Zayed was a champion of the environment long before it became fashionable, and this island, which means "sons of Yas", is testament to that. One of the largest natural reserve islands in the world, it has been reforested with almost two million trees, which are home to more than 150 species of birds. The Arabian oryx that roam the land here were part of a captive breeding program started by Sheikh Zayed; the UAE is home to two-thirds of the world's population of this horned gazelle. And the reserve has lost count of the number of peacocks, since the environment is ideal for them to breed. You can also see South African flamingoes on the waters near the 64-room Anantara Desert Islands Resort & Spa. Sir Bani Yas is also a popular place for archeologists as it has relics dating from the Stone Age, including a Christian monastery from the pre-Islamic age. Located 8km from the mainland, the island is accessible by plane or ferry, which leaves from Jebel Al Dhana.

Psst...

Getting to the island is quite an exciting activity because it will require that you either drive to the western region and then take a jeti at one of their stops at Jebel Dhana, or fly.

A flight can be booked via the Anantara hotel, however they only depart on the following days: Tuesday, Thursday, Friday and Saturday. It costs approximately Dhs300 for one way, per person and additional 16% service charge.

Futaisi Island

www.futaisi.com; 02 666 6601; Al Mina Bateen

In the old area of Abu Dhabi is a hidden gem that has an interesting history and an amazing variety of wildlife. The 50-kilometer island dates back hundreds of years and was the source of drinking water because of its geology. There is a restored fort that shows the history of the place. Take a bike tour and see the Arabian horses in stables or gazelles running around. In the water you might see sea turtles or flamingoes. This is a popular place for private cruises. Many expats visit for barbecues or private gatherings.

Samaliya Island

www.torath.ae; 02 558 1544

A fascinating island to explore, Samaliya Island is positioned about 12 kilometers off the Abu Dhabi coast. Samaliya has an impressive marine environment due to its rich biodiversity, which makes it the ideal place to discover rare marine plants, mangroves, fish, turtles, seabirds and even snakes.

Emirates National Auto Museum

www.enam.ae; 050 829 3952; on the way to Hameem, Western Region

The Emirates National Auto Museum is a private collection of cars that belong to Sheikh Hamad bin Hamdan Al Nahyan. It's well worth a visit to see the 200 or so cars, including the enormous Dodge pickup (which still works) that is in the *Guinness World Records* book. The 50-ton Dodge even has four bedrooms inside. The museum also has the seven Mercedes that Sheikh Hamad bought in the 1980s, one for each day of the week and each with a different color interior. Not too hard to see why they call him the Rainbow Sheikh.

The museum's regular hours are on Friday and Saturday from 8am until 5pm. I would recommend calling Arbit Sinkh to check first; however, he is very flexible about other days if given advance notice.

Liwa and the Empty Quarter
www.algharbia.ae; Western Region

Liwa is located 150 kilometers away from Abu Dhabi, but is well worth the drive. Spectacular sand dunes, scattered villages and the vast Empty Quarter (more than 650,000 square kilometers) are awe-inspiring. There are spots for paragliding, camping, motorbiking and ATV racing. Take a drive out to Tal Moreeb, which is a must-see huge dune. This is my favorite place to watch the stars because of the clear skies; it's so calm in the middle of the desert and you can lose count of how many shooting stars you see. There are two new hotels offering unforgettable experiences in the desert: Qasr Al Sarab (02 886 2088) and the Tilal Liwa (02 894 6111).

Desert tours

A fun way to see the vast sand dunes of the UAE's interior and get a sense of our ancestral hospitality is to go on a desert tour. There are many operators you can use or you can just rent a car and a driver. If you decide to do it alone, make sure you are prepared. The desert is, well, deserted. You don't want to be stranded out there on your own.

If you choose a tour, a driver will pick up your party in the city at about 3pm and drive you an hour out of town to the desert. First, you will be able to mingle with some tame, friendly camels. Then, under the beauty of sunset, it's dune-bashing time. Don't worry, it's not as violent as it sounds. Bashing simply means driving up and around the dunes, sort of like a being on a roller coaster. Your driver will make a brief stop for you to lose your lunch (kidding!) and take some pictures. At the top of the dune, many people try sand boarding. I remember having an awesome time.

Psst...

Some tour operators will escort you to a re-creation of a local camp. They offer an "authentic" experience in which you can have your picture taken in traditional Emirati dress and experience local cuisine. They might offer more exotic Arabian touches such as shisha and belly dancers, but remember that these things are not native to the UAE or our culture.

Also...

A tour operator will take care of you. But if you decide to go on your own it is important that you follow certain rules. Carry a battery-operated flashlight. Keep your mobile fully charged and carry a portable charger. Let someone know you're heading out to the desert and what time you'll be back. Hire a local guide who knows the area well. Carry enough food and, most importantly, enough water to last you the entire trip.

Ask Ali farm

www.embracearabia.com; 02 641 9914

The UAE, much to the surprise of most visitors, is an agricultural country. Most of the Bedouins of the Arabian Peninsula used to live in oases and cultivate date palms and breed livestock for survival. Sometimes, I show people around my personal farm to give them a sense of the Arabian lifestyle as it was and how it came to be.

Just 45 minutes away from Abu Dhabi, the farm is a refreshing retreat. It is spread over one square kilometer and features a huge palm garden, green fields, and a traditional farmhouse. There is a classic majlis and a terrace overlooking the plantation. The farmers offer true Arabian hospitality and explain their way of life, how their fruit and vegetables are cultivated, and how the traditional irrigation method known as falaj works.

This is where my Saluki, chickens, horse and goats stay, as it is quite spacious and the environment is suitable for them.

Al Ain

Al Ain is known for its greenery as well as its rocky mountain ranges. It has lots to offer that can't be found anywhere else in the country. There are 4,000-year-old tombs, a 175-year-old Al Nahyan family fort, and the UAE's only remaining traditional camel market. I would recommend you spend some time in the tranquil shade surrounded by the palm trees of the oasis. Many of the palm plantations are working farms so you can see the ancient falaj irrigation system in action. Then go and see some haggling at its best at the camel market before going to Al Jahili Fort, where Sheikh Zayed was born. Stop off at the Al Ain Palace Museum where Sheikh Zayed lived when he was in Al Ain, and the Hili Archeological Gardens. Enjoy spectacular views of the area from the summit of the UAE's second-tallest mountain, Jebel Hafeet (1,180 meters). Stop at the bottom to dip your toes in the hot springs of Green Mubazzarah or pop into the Mercure Grand Hotel at the top for lunch on the terrace.

Dubai

www.dubaitourism.ae

Chances are that while you are here you will visit our beautiful sister destination just down the highway. The first thing you will notice is the size of Dubai – the skyscrapers are massive! Discover the Jumeirah Beach area, close to the distinctive sail-shaped Burj al Arab hotel, which in turn is near the man-made island The Palm. The newest addition to Dubai's tourism industry is the Burj Khalifa, the tallest building in the world.

In the older end of town you can take a ride on an abra across Dubai Creek. Visit the gold souq and Dubai Museum, which has lifelike recreations of Bedouin times. Grab a bite to eat and explore the art in the Bastakiya area.

A visit to Dubai wouldn't be complete without a visit to the malls, including Mall of the Emirates, where you can ski even when it is 40°C outside and Dubai Mall, one of the biggest in the world. I have just launched *Ask Ali: A guide to Dubai*, so be sure to get your copy to get the full scoop on the "City of Life".

Sharjah

www.sharjahtourism.ae

Smile, you're in Sharjah. That's how the signs welcome you to
this emirate that is famous for its museums. Although it is only a
20-minute drive from Dubai, you could spend a weekend and not
get through all the exhibitions. Of note are the maritime, heritage,
art and calligraphy museums. The emirate also features some fine
souqs and markets, including a wonderful fish market and it is also
a great place to buy furniture. The Blue Souq is arguably the best
place in the entire country to buy Persian carpets and pashminas.

Visit the beautiful Qanat al Qasba and get a taste of the Sharjawi
way to relax in the open air, with games for the family and
delicious street food. They organize different festivals and events
throughout the year; visit www.qaq.ae for all the details.

Ajman

Ajman is the smallest of the seven emirates and has almost no oil wealth of its own. This is why Ajman was forced to concentrate on establishing small-scale industries. For example, there is a wharf, where fiberglass dhows are built using traditional methods. The emirate also has industries recycling scrap metal and a large printing press, where telephone books and Government documents are printed. For visitors, it has a beautiful view of the ocean and plenty of cafes to take that view in. You might note the color orange in this emirate, which represents their soccer club.

The beaches in Ajman are bustling with sports activities – you always see guys playing volleyball or football. They are the best place to hang out also due to the nearby shops and cafes.

Umm al Qaiwain

This emirate is rightly known for its calmness and is a great place to get away and relax, maybe in one of its famous chalets. A great one to visit is the Flamingo Beach Resort (06 765 0000). But there's also fun to be had: the Gulf's largest water park, Dreamland, is here, as well as skydiving, which is offered through the UAQ Aeroclub.

Canoeing is another "must do" activity in this wonderful emirate as it is scattered with small mangrove islands that are inhabited with flamingos and other sea birds.

Ras al Khaimah

www.raktourism.com

Only an hour away from Dubai, this area was once known as the Pirate Coast because of the high seas antics that took place off its shores. Don't worry, the locals are very friendly these days. Ras al Khaimah is home to the oldest seaport in the region, a museum, the old town and the starkly beautiful Hajar Mountains, the highest in the country.

Rain is common and it even snowed on the summits one recent winter, though it quickly melted away (hey, it still counts). There are interesting caves, hiking trails, untouched pools and some beautiful beach resorts to enjoy.

Out and about

Fujairah

www.fujairah-tourism.gov.ae

To me, as an Emirati, you gotta love Fujairah. Pack the picnic supplies and spend a weekend with the family in this emirate known for its natural resources. There are two famous wadis (valleys) nearby: Wadi Siji, which is about 50km north of Fujairah city, and Wadi al Hail, which starts in Al Hail and extends for 15km to the south-west of the emirate. Other places to visit include the 400-year-old Al Bidya Mosque and Fujairah Fort, the strategically located mud brick structure in old Fujairah that dates back to 1670. In the mountains is the town of Masafi, known for its freshwater springs that provide the bottled water found nationwide. On Fridays, check out Al Jumaa market, one of my favourite markets, a small outdoor souq where you can buy fresh vegetables and fruit, garden plants, carpets, pottery and toys. The market is open all week, although Friday is the most popular day.

Glossary: Arabic phrases

Although English is widely spoken and taught in schools, you may encounter some people who do not speak it. Arabic is the main language spoken by Emiratis, along with other Arabs who reside in the UAE.

Most of the Arabic phrases below are in the Emirati dialect as opposed to classical Arabic. That's not to say that if you were to use these in Saudi Arabia, you wouldn't be understood.

Greetings & manners

Peace be upon you	As salamu alaykum (this phrase is short for As salamu alaykum wa ra hamatu allahi wa baraktuh).
Response	Wa alaykum as salam
Hello	Marhaba
Response	Ya marhaba / Ahlen
How are you?	(Kaif or Chaif) el hal
I'm well, thanks be to God	Bekhair Alhamdulillah
How is your health?	Kaif al seha
I'm well, thanks be to God	Bekhair Alhamdulillah
Good or OK	Tamaam
Not good	Mosh bekhair
My pleasure	Bekul suroor
Thank you	Shukran
	Mashkoor (M)
	Mashkoora (F)
	Teslam (M)
	Teslameen (F)
You're welcome	El 'Aafu
Response	Allah ysalmak (M)
	Allah ysalmech (F)

What is your name?	Shu esmak? (M)
	Shu esmech? (F)
My name is	Ana esmi
How old are you?	Kam omrak (M)
	Kam omrech (F)
Where are you from?	Ent men wain? (M)
	Enti men wain? (F)
I am from	Ana min
Pleased to meet you	Fursa sa'eeda or Etsharafna
Response	Elsharaf lee
Goodbye	Ma' asallama
Good luck	Bel tawfiq or Muwafaq
Good night	Tesbah ala khair (M)
	Tesbaheen ala khair (F)
May God bless you	Baraka Allah feek (M)
	Baraka Allah feech (F)
May God accept your prayers	Taqabal Allah salatakom
God grant you goodness	Jazak Allah khair
Have a blessed Eid	Eedkom embarak
Happy Eid	Eid saeed
Have a blessed Ramadan	Ramadan Kareem
Happy new year	Kul aaam wa anta be khayr (M)
	Kul aaam wa anti be khayr (F)
Congratulations	Mabrook
Response	Allah yebarek feek (M)
	Allah yebarek feech (F)
Condolences	Al baqeya fe hayatak (M)
	Al baqeyah fe hayatech (F)
Response	Hayatak al baqiyah (M)
	Hayatek al baqiyah (F)
Excuse me	Ann ethnik
Sorry	Asif (M) Asifa (F)
	Esmahli (M) Esmahili (F)

231

Please	Law samaht
It's OK	Ma'leh or Ma'laish
Yes	Na'am or Aywah
No	Laa
Bon appétit	Bel Aafiya or Bel Hana welshefa
Good on you	Ahsant (M) Ahsanti (F)

Getting there

Where?	Wain?
What?	Shu?
When?	Mata?
Why?	Laish?
How?	Kaifa?
Who?	Meen?
I want to go to	Aba aseer
How do I go to?	Kef aseer?
Show me the way please	Delni ala tareeq men fadhlak (M)
	Deleeni ala tareeq men fadhlech (F)
What street is this?	Hadha ay share'e
North	Shimal
South	Junoob
East	Sharq
West	Gharb
Right	Yamin
Left	Yasar
Straight	Seeda
In front	Jeddam
Back	Wara
Opposite	Muqa-bel
Near	Gareeb
Far	Ba'eed
Stop	Wagaf

Wait here	Etraya hnee
Car	Sayyarah
Taxi	Sayyarat al ojrah
Bus	Baas
Boat	Qarib
Airplane	Tayyarah

Time & days

What time is it?	El sa'a kam
It is now	Elsa'a alheen
1 o'clock	Wahda
1:15	Wahda wa rob'o
1:30	Wahda wa nos
1:45	Ethneen ela rob'o (quarter to two)
2 o'clock	Thentain
Day	Youm
Week	Osbo'o
Month	Shahar
Year	Sanah
Sunday	El Ahad
Monday	El Ethnain
Tuesday	El Thulatha
Wednesday	El Arbe'aa
Thursday	El Khamees
Friday	El Juma'a
Saturday	El sabt
Today	Elyoum
Tomorrow	Bacher
After tomorrow	Ba'ad bacher
Yesterday	Amss
Before yesterday	Gabl elbarha
Now	Alheen
Later	Baaden

Money matters

Money	Bezat / Floos
Cents	Fils
ATM	Alat sahab
Checkbook	Daftar chekat
Where can I buy?	Mn wain agdar ashtiree
How much is this?	Cham hadha?
How many pieces?	Cham habba
Too expensive	Wayed ghali
Cheap	Rakhees
Reasonable price	Se'er ma'agool

Numbers

Zero	Sefr
One	Wahed
Two	Ethnen
Three	Thalaath
Four	Arba'a
Five	Khamsa
Six	Sitta
Seven	Saba'a
Eight	Thamanyah
Nine	Tes'a
Ten	A'ashra
Hundred	Emyah
Thousand	Alf
Million	Malyoon

Places

Airport	Mattar
Port	Mina
Hotel	Funduq

Resort	Montajaa
House	Bait
Apartment	Sheqah
Tent	Khaimah
Tower	Burj
Company	Sharekah
Museum	Mat-haf
Mosque	Masjid
Church	Kanesah
Cemetery	Maqbara
Embassy	Safara
Hospital	Mostashfa
Clinic	Iyadah
Restaurant	Mataam
Shopping mall	Markaz tejari / Mall
Market	Souq
Shop	Mahal
Beauty salon	Salon eltajmeel
Grocery	Baqqala
Laundromat	Doobi
Vegetable market	Souq el khodra
Fish market	Souq el samak
Farm	Ezba
Desert	Sahra
School	Madrasa
College	Kulliyah
University	Jaam'ah
Police department	Markaz elshurta
Court	Mahkama
Gas station	Sheeshat petrol
Car wash	Maghsala
Bus station	Mahattat el bas
Street	Share'a

Roundabout	Dawwar
Bridge	Jesr
Entrance	Madkhal
Exit	Makhraj
Neighborhood	Sha'biyah
Country	Bilad
City	Madinah
Sea	Bahar
Island	Jazeerah

Miscellaneous

Beautiful	Jameel (M)
	Jameela (F)
Precious	Ghali
Generous	Kareem
Stingy	Bakheel
Smart	Dhaki
Crazy	Khbal
Healthy	Sehi
Sick	Mayhood / Mareedh (M)
	Mayhooda / Mareedha (F)
Religious	Mutadayen
Religion	Diyana
Culture	Thaqafa
Education	Taaleem
Impossible	Mustaheel
Replica	Taqleed
Coffee	Gahwa
Tea	Shai
Nationality	Jinsiyah
Police	Shurta
Permit	Rokhsa

License	Lesan
Ambulance	Is'aaf
Newspaper	Jareeda
Magazine	Majjalah
Visa	Taasheera
Residency	Iqamah
Passport	Jawaz
Palm tree	Nakhl
Date	Tamr
Falcon	Saqr
Tip	Bakhsheesh
Stand up	Ewgaf (M)
	Ewgafi (F)
Sit down	Eyles (M)
	Yelsi (F)
Calm down	Haddi
Move	Khooz (M)
	Khoozi (F)
Open	Battel (M)
	Battli (F)
Close	Bannad (M)
	Banndi (F)
Friend	Sadeeqi (M)
	Sadeeqti (F)
Colleague	Zameel (M)
	Zameelti (F)
My boss	Mudeer (M)
	Mudeerti (F)
Wedding	Ers
Bride	Aroos
Groom	Maeris

Numbers as Arabic letters

If you want to impress your friends when texting them, try to use these letters in anglicized Arabic conversations over the internet or texts, and you will blow them away.

These are basically letters that are not available in the Latin alphabet, therefore they have been substituted by numbers. It was previously used by teenagers when internet chat rooms became popular. It is not used in the corporate world, however it is understood and used by everybody in the Arab world.

Letter=Number
Aain = 3
Ghain = '3
Kha = 5
Taa = 6
Ssad = 9
Dha = '9
Haa = 7

Example
Ali = **3**li
Gharbiya = **'3**arbiya
Khalifa = **5**alifa
Tarzan = **6**arazan
Sefr = **9**efr
Abu **Dh**abi = Abu **'9**abi
Mo**h**ammed = Mo**7**ammed

Detailed instructions

When typing Arabic letters in English, these letters will have to be replaced by the numbers that correspond to them in shape:

- Number **2** substitutes the Arabic letter "آ" or "ء". It's pronounced as "a" in "amber" and is also used for a glottal stop, "ء", as in the English word "uh-oh".

- Number **7** substitutes the Arabic letter "ح". Its pronunciation is a soft "haa", this one being breathy.

- Number **5** substitutes the Arabic letter "خ". It's pronounced as "kh" but in a heavier way, just like the German "ch".

- Number **9** substitutes the Arabic letter "ص". It's a heavier "ss" and achieved by the tongue touching the roof of the mouth.

- Number **'9** substitutes the Arabic letter "ض"or "ظ". It's pronounced as an emphatic "dha" with the apostrophe as the dot.

- Number **6** substitues the Arabic letter "ط". This letter is pronounced as an emphatic "tta".

- Number **3** replaces the Arabic letter "ع". It's pronounced as a heavy "ah" by slightly pushing your tongue into the back of your throat.

- The number **3'** is used for the Arabic letter "غ". This letter is pronounced as "gha" like how the French pronounce their "r" with the apostrophe as the dot.

Common Arabic terms

In these terms and phrases you may notice that words are spelled differently in other books. Don't worry about it, because there is no correct way of spelling it. The purpose is to have the pronounciation as close as possible to the original Arabic word.

Abaya – A long black gown worn on top of clothes by women in the Gulf

Abra – A wooden boat used for transportation (water taxi)

Adab – Manners

Adhaan – Call to prayer

Barjeel – Wind tower

Bukhoor – Arabic incense burned on coal to give a nice smell

Shway shway – Slowly slowly

Dhow – A sailing vessel, much bigger than an abra

Endok inta – A sarcastic way of saying "are you serious" or "here you go"

Falak Tayeb – A way of saying "whatever you wish"

Fedaitak / Fedaitech – Term of endearment meaning you'll sacrifice your life for them

Dubai "the city of life" – Edbai dar elha

Gahfiya – A white cap worn underneath a ghutra so it doesn't slip

Ghutra – A white head scarf worn by Arab men

Habibi / Habibti – Meaning "my love"

HH / HE – His or Her Highness / His or Her Excellency

Hajj – Muslim pilgrimage to Mecca (Makkah) during the lunar Arabic month of Dhul Hijjah

Halal – According to Islamic law, opposite of haram

Haram – Forbidden in Islam

Hawala – Money transfer

Hawwiya – Identity

Hayati – Describing a loved one as "my life"

Huwy – Courtyard

Iftar – Breaking fast

Imam – Man who leads prayer in the mosque

Kachra – Rubbish

Kandoura – White dress worn by men in the Gulf

Khaleej – Gulf countries

Khanjar – Curved dagger

Khor – Creek

Mashallah – Said when in awe of something, similar to "touch wood"

Mufti – Religious scholar

Niqab – A piece of cloth worn by women to cover their face

Ogal – A black cord that secures the ghutra in place

Omrah – Muslim pilgrimage to Mecca (Makkah) during any time of the year

Qibla – The direction toward Mecca (Makkah), used when praying or burying a dead Muslim

Quran – The holy book of Islam

Riba – Usury (forbidden in Islam to charge interest on loans)

Sawm – Fasting

Sheikh – Leader of a country, religious scholar or an elderly man worthy of respect

Sheikha – Female version of a sheikh

Sheila – A rectangular scarf worn by women to cover their hair

Shu el akhbar – Common phrase for asking "what's your news"

Tagiya – Alternate name for cap worn underneath a ghutra (see Gahfiya on previous page)

Wasta – The connections you use from knowing influential people

Wodhu – Ablution ritual before prayers

Yallah – Come on or let's go

Psst... Don't forget!

Connect online

If you want to get to know our master's day-to-day activities and get his updates, please follow him on Facebook and Twitter:
www.facebook.com/AskAliOfficialFanPage
www.twitter.com/AskAli

Dubai guide

When you decide to visit our neighbour emirate, make sure you pick up a copy of *Ask Ali: A guide to Dubai* for more cultural tips and local knowledge on Ali's favorite things to do, places to go and eat when you are there. Plus you can meet me, Mau; I'm Ali's favourite pet in the Dubai guide!

Do you have any comments, feedback or recommendations about things you think I should know?
Please feel free to drop me an e-mail at ali@ask-ali.com and I will review it, insha'allah.